SCHOLASTIC

BOOK OF 2015 WORLD RECORDS

BY JENIFER CORR MORSE
A GEORGIAN BAY BOOK

SCHOLASTIC INC.

To Isabelle Nicole—May you always find wonder in the world.
—JCM

CREATED AND PRODUCED BY GEORGIAN BAY LLC
Copyright © 2014 by Georgian Bay LLC

GEORGIAN BAY STAFF
Bruce S. Glassman, Executive Editor
Jenifer Corr Morse, Author
Joe Bernier, Designer

ISBN 978-0-545-67950-3

10 9 8 7 6 5 4 3 2 1   14 15 16 17

Printed in the U.S.A.   40
First edition, November 2014

Cover design by Will Denton
Deb Cohn-Orbach, Photo Editor

In most cases, the graphs in this book represent the top five record holders in each category. However, in some graphs, we have chosen to list well-known or common people, places, animals, or things that will help you better understand how extraordinary the record holder is. These may not be the top five in the category. Additionally, some graphs have fewer than five entries because so few people or objects reflect the necessary criteria.

Due to the publication date, the majority of statistics is current as of June 2014.

Contents

Science & Technology Records

Radio Ramblings

Pandora radio—a free Internet station that personalizes music— has about 175 million registered users, with more than 75 million actively listening regularly. It accounts for about 9.1 percent of the US radio market. The app logged about 16.7 billion listening hours during 2013. Since Pandora began in 2000, it has collected more than 100,000 tracks in their impressive library.

Serious Screen Time

Some 56 percent of US adults own smartphones, and popularity is growing across the globe. In fact, about 937 million smartphones shipped worldwide in 2013. Average US users check their phones about 150 times a day. About 96 percent of them text, and mobile users send about 678 texts monthly. About 17 percent of global web traffic comes from cell phone users.

Socially Acceptable

In the US, people have made social media the top Internet activity, spending about 37 minutes a day browsing and updating profiles. About 60 percent of social media time is spent on mobile devices. Some people check in the car (31 percent), some in restaurants (30 percent), and some even check in the bathroom (21 percent). Facebook is the most popular site, logging about 114 billion minutes a month in the US.

Scoping Out the Stars

The Arecibo Observatory in Puerto Rico is a national research center operated by Cornell University, and operates the world's largest single-dish radio telescope. The telescope's dish measures 1,000 feet (305 m) in diameter and is made up of 38,778 aluminum plates. It is used to study several branches of astronomy.

Hold on Tight

Verruckt Meg-A-Blaster— the world's tallest, fastest, and steepest water slide— opened at Schlitterbahn in Kansas City, Kansas, in 2014. Brave riders climb 264 steps to the top of the slide to board a four-person inflatable raft. Then they zoom at speeds of 65 miles (104 km) an hour down a five-story drop. The drop is taller than Niagara Falls and steeper than a ski slope.

Plane Powerful

The giant Boeing 747-8 Intercontinental can carry up to 467 passengers, and has the electrical capacity to power 480,000 thirty-two-inch flat-screen TVs. The plane has a top speed of 614 miles (988 km) per hour. It can cover three soccer stadiums in 1 second, and complete a standard marathon in 2.5 minutes.

Going Up?

One of the fastest elevators in the world is housed in the Taipei 101 office building in Taiwan. The elevator travels at 37.7 miles (60.7 km) per hour, or 3,313 feet (1,010 m) per minute. The journey from the ground to the roof of the 1670-foot (509 m) building lasts just 30 seconds. The elevator cost more than $2 million.

bestselling family video game

Pokémon X/Y

Pokémon X/Y sold more than 9.9 million copies in 2013. Produced for Nintendo 3DS, both the X and Y versions were released in October of that year. As with other games in the series, X and Y are about Ash Ketchum and his friends, and their efforts to train Pokémon. However, the game takes place in the region of Kalos, and introduces 74 new Pokémon. Also new, trainers can use Mega Evolution to further develop Pokémon that are fully evolved. The main missions in Pokémon X/Y are to defeat the evil Team Flare, and challenge the Pokémon League Champion. Although the games feature a very similar plot, they can be purchased and played independently.

bestselling family video games

units sold in 2013, in millions

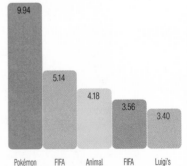

9.94	5.14	4.18	3.56	3.40
Pokémon X/Y (3DS)	FIFA Soccer 14 (PS3)	Animal Crossing: New Leaf (3DS)	FIFA Soccer 14 (X360)	Luigi's Mansion: Dark Moon (3DS)

bestselling gaming console

3DS

The most popular gaming console in 2013 was Nintendo 3DS, which sold more than 14 million units. Gamers can enjoy all the 3-D effects without glasses. The console has two screens, and its 3-D technology supports movies and videos. It also features three cameras, an activity log, an Internet browser, and access to the Nintendo Network. When it was first released in February 2011, 3DS had the highest one-day sales of any Nintendo portable gaming device. During the first week of release, about 440,000 units were sold.

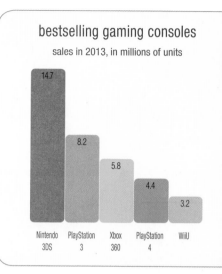

bestselling gaming consoles
sales in 2013, in millions of units

Nintendo 3DS	PlayStation 3	Xbox 360	PlayStation 4	WiiU
14.7	8.2	5.8	4.4	3.2

family show with the highest average tweets

Glee

Fans of *Glee*—the very popular Fox comedy/drama about a high school glee club—are very social when the show airs each week. An average of 238,000 tweets went out per episode in 2013. The glee club of William McKinley High School is known as New Directions, and its members have included Rachel Berry (Lea Michelle), Kurt Hummel (Chris Coffer), and Mercedes Jones (Amber Riley). The series also stars Jane Lynch as Sue Sylvester and Matthew Morrison as Will Shuester. *Glee* has been nominated for 21 Emmy Awards and won 4 of them. It's also picked up 4 Golden Globe Awards, including Best Television Series in 2010.

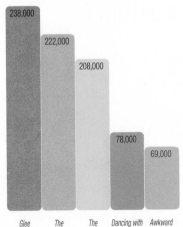

family shows with the highest average tweets

average number of tweets per episode in 2013

Glee	The X Factor	The Voice	Dancing with the Stars	Awkward
238,000	222,000	208,000	78,000	69,000

most-visited social site

Facebook

More than 800 million unique visitors click on the Facebook website each month. That's more than the next four social sites combined. Facebook was founded by Mark Zuckerberg in 2004 as a way for Harvard students to keep in touch. Ten years later, Facebook has about 1.28 billion registered users, and about 757 million log-ons every day. Every minute of the day, about 4.75 billion pieces of content are shared. People spend an average of 8.3 hours on Facebook each month. There are around 150 billion friend connections, and 4.5 billion "likes" per day.

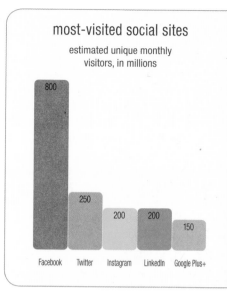

most-visited social sites

estimated unique monthly visitors, in millions

Facebook	Twitter	Instagram	LinkedIn	Google Plus+
800	250	200	200	150

most-used search engine

Google

About 67 percent of people browsing the Internet choose Google as their search engine. Google is the world's largest online index of websites. In addition, Google offers email, maps, news, and financial services, among others. Headquartered in California's Silicon Valley, the company runs hundreds of thousands of servers around the globe. A "googol" is a 1 followed by 100 zeros, and the site was named after the term to indicate its mission to organize the virtually infinite amount of information on the Web.

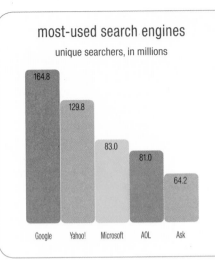

most-used search engines
unique searchers, in millions

Google	Yahoo!	Microsoft	AOL	Ask
164.8	129.8	83.0	81.0	64.2

most-visited website

Google

The most-visited website in the world is Google, which gets more than 164 million unique page views per month. Created by Stanford grad students Larry Page and Sergey Brin in 1998, Google has indexed 30 trillion pages. Google performs about 100 billion searches each month. There are more than 425 million people using Gmail, the website's e-mail feature. Over the years, Google has acquired many impressive companies, including YouTube, Android, DoubleClick, and Blogger. Google employs more than 50,000 people worldwide.

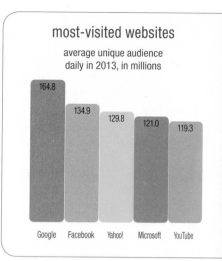

most-visited websites

average unique audience daily in 2013, in millions

Google	Facebook	Yahoo!	Microsoft	YouTube
164.8	134.9	129.8	121.0	119.3

most successful shopping site

Amazon.com

Shopping megasite Amazon.com made up more than 10 percent of the US market share in 2013. The site, which got its start selling books, now offers everything from clothes and electronics to food and furniture. Founded by Jeffrey Bezos in 1994, it is headquartered in Seattle, Washington. The company also has separate websites in countries including Japan, Canada, the United Kingdom, Germany, and France.

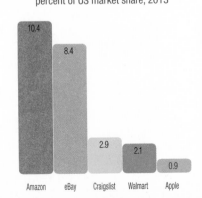

most successful shopping sites
percent of US market share, 2013

Amazon	eBay	Craigslist	Walmart	Apple
10.4	8.4	2.9	2.1	0.9

top-streaming site

Netflix

When people want to stream shows and movies, more than 52 percent of them turn to Netflix. That's more than the next two services combined. Customers can watch on their computers, smartphones, and tablets, or through their TVs if they have a game console or other device connected to the Internet. Netflix has more than 44 million streaming members throughout 40 countries, and streams more than 1 billion hours of shows and movies per month. In 2013, Netflix became the first online streaming site to earn Emmy nominations for three of its web series—*Arrested Development, House of Cards,* and *Hemlock Grove.*

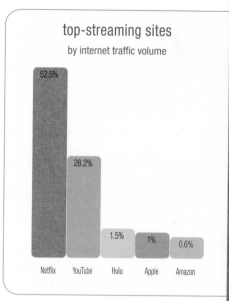

top-streaming sites
by internet traffic volume

52.5%	28.2%	1.5%	1%	0.6%
Netflix	YouTube	Hulu	Apple	Amazon

1 800 382 639

PSY - GANGNAM STYLE

E (강남스타일) M/V

1,808,286,535

most-viewed YouTube video

"Gangnam Style"

South Korean singer PSY released "Gangnam Style" in July 2012, and it has since become the most-viewed video on YouTube with more than 1.8 billion hits. In fact, it had more than 500,000 views on its first day. In December 2012, it averaged about 76.4 views per second. It was the first single off his sixth album, *PSY 6 (Six Rules), Part 1*. The song, which debuted at the top of the South Korean charts, describes the trendy lifestyle of the Gangnam region in Seoul. "Gangnam Style" won Best Video at the South Korea 2012 MTV Video Music Awards.

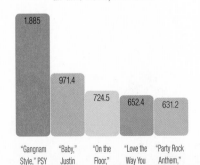

most-viewed YouTube videos

all-time views, in millions

"Gangnam Style," PSY	"Baby," Justin Bieber	"On the Floor," Jennifer Lopez	"Love the Way You Lie," Eminem	"Party Rock Anthem," LMFAO
1,885	971.4	724.5	652.4	631.2

top-grossing mobile game app

Candy Crush Saga

Each day, people around the world spend about $910,000 playing Candy Crush Saga! Players try their luck at matching at least three of the same kind of candy in a row, hoping to make enough disappear to reach the goal of the level. Although the game can be downloaded for free, players can buy extra lives when they run out of the 5 lives that are provided at the start of each game. Players who are stuck on a level can buy additional candy in hopes of advancing to the next level. The game was released on Facebook in April 2012, and about 46 million users play each month. In November 2012, Candy Crush Saga was released on smartphones and tablets.

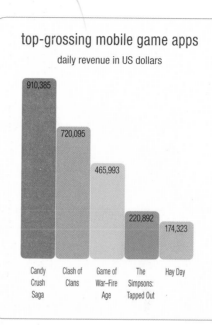

top-grossing mobile game apps
daily revenue in US dollars

Candy Crush Saga	Clash of Clans	Game of War–Fire Age	The Simpsons: Tapped Out	Hay Day
910,385	720,095	465,993	220,892	174,323

product with the most Facebook fans

Coca-Cola

Coca-Cola is the most popular product on Facebook, with more than 78 million fans. On the page, fans can post and read stories, explore products, and check out the latest photos. The company has acquired some impressive statistics during its 128 years in business. Coca-Cola produces more than 3,500 different types of beverages, which are sold in 200 countries throughout the world. Each day, about 1.7 billion servings of Coca-Cola products are enjoyed. In addition to its cola products, the company also produces A&W, Crush, Dasani, Hi-C, Minute Maid, Nestea, and many others.

products with the most Facebook fans

number of fans, in millions

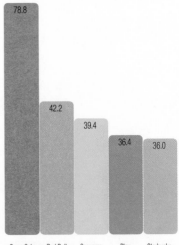

Coca-Cola	Red Bull	Converse All Stars	Play Station	Starbucks
78.8	42.2	39.4	36.4	36.0

most-searched image on google

"Funny Pictures"

People surfing the Internet like to laugh, especially at photos. Browsers using Google image search made "funny pictures" the most-searched image on the site in 2013. This search pulls up everything from photos of humorous pets to laughing babies. There are also links to websites that have all types of funny images and stories. In fact, that search pulls up about 895 million hits in less than a second. Each month, Google performs about 12.47 billion searches. In fact, more than half of all Internet users end up typing in their own names to see what Google can find on them.

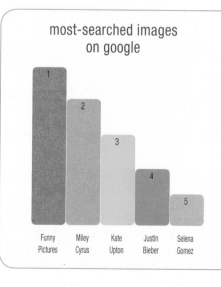

most-searched images on google

1	2	3	4	5
Funny Pictures	Miley Cyrus	Kate Upton	Justin Bieber	Selena Gomez

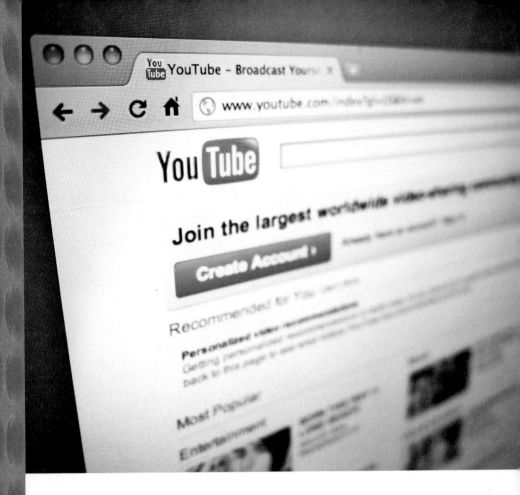

most-visited video site

YouTube

When Web surfers are looking for videos, the majority log on to YouTube. With more than 128 million unique visitors per month, YouTube can turn everyday people into Internet stars. On the site, anyone can upload their own videos for the world to see. YouTube gets about 3 billion views per day. Each minute, about 48 hours of video are uploaded to the site. In fact, more video is uploaded to YouTube in one month than the three largest broadcast networks could create in 60 years. About 500 years' worth of YouTube video is shared on Facebook each day, and another 700 YouTube videos are shared on Twitter each minute.

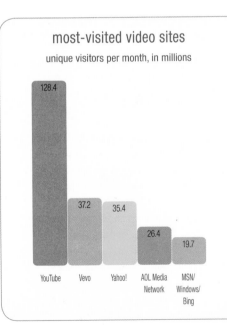

most-visited video sites
unique visitors per month, in millions

Site	Visitors
YouTube	128.4
Vevo	37.2
Yahoo!	35.4
AOL Media Network	26.4
MSN/ Windows/ Bing	19.7

country with the highest Twitter usage

Saudi Arabia

Saudi Arabia leads the world in active Twitter users with 33 percent of its population sending out tweets. While other countries have a much larger number of users, most are not actively sending out tweets on a regular basis. In fact, Saudi Arabia only makes up about 4.1 percent of the Twitter market. But the fast-growing popularity of smartphones makes it easy to access the Internet from anywhere, and about 60 percent of Saudis take advantage of this. The country also leads the world in the number of minutes spent online with a mobile device.

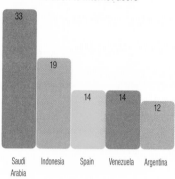

countries with the highest Twitter usage

percentage of active Twitter users in relation to Internet users

Saudi Arabia	Indonesia	Spain	Venezuela	Argentina
33	19	14	14	12

celebrity with the most Twitter followers

Katy Perry

More than 52 million fans follow Katy Perry on Twitter since she joined the site in February 2009. The singer has sent out about 5,400 tweets since joining and averages 2 per day. In November 2013, @katyperry became the most popular celebrity Twitter handle. Three months later, Perry tweeted to her "Katycats" to celebrate becoming the first person to surpass 50 million followers. Perry owes some of her popularity to the 2014 Grammy Awards, where she performed her hit "Dark Horse." After the show aired, she picked up an additional 800,000 followers!

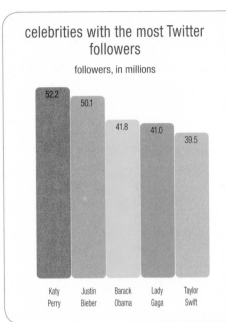

celebrities with the most Twitter followers

followers, in millions

52.2	50.1	41.8	41.0	39.5
Katy Perry	Justin Bieber	Barack Obama	Lady Gaga	Taylor Swift

THE

PRISMATIC

WORLD TOUR

Katy Perry ✓

@katyperry

LET THE LIGHT IN. PRISM. OUT NOW!

REALITY · katyperry.com

TWEETS	FOLLOWING	FOLLOWERS	
5,486	136	52.2M	👤 **Follow**

Tweets All / **No replies**

Katy Perry @katyperry · Apr 13

Sand is the new dry shampoo. #coachella

Expand   ↩ Reply   ⟲ Retweet   ★ Favorite   ••• More

Katy Perry @katyperry · Apr 13

most active Twitter moment

Castle in the Sky airing

The annual television screening of the 28-year-old animated Japanese film classic *Castle in the Sky* averaged 143,199 tweets per second! When *Castle in the Sky* aired in December 2013 in Japan, fans were encouraged to tweet the word "balse" to help Pazu and Sheeta—the main characters—cast a spell. Clearly fans responded. The film was created in Japan by Hayao Miyazaki and was released in 1986. It was later rereleased in English by Disney in 1999. The English version featured the voices of James Van Der Beek, Anna Paquin, Cloris Leachman, and Mark Hamill.

most active Twitter moments
tweets per second

143,199	33,388	25,088	16,197	15,358
Castle in the Sky airing, 2013	Japanese New Year, 2013	Castle in the Sky airing, 2011	Japanese New Year, 2012	European Soccer Championship Final, 2012

most popular blog

Huffington Post

The Huffington Post blog pulls in about 110 million unique visitors each month—more than the next top four blogs combined! The Huffington Post website includes current events and news stories from around the world, and its blogs have similar content. Some of their content categories include comedy, college, style, technology, and politics. They also have a blogger dedicated to teens and teen interests. Sometimes even celebrities, athletes, and politicians contribute a blog. The Huffington Post has won two Webby Awards for the Best Political Blog, and in 2012, it picked up a Pulitzer Prize.

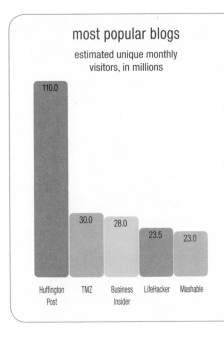

most popular blogs

estimated unique monthly visitors, in millions

Huffington Post	TMZ	Business Insider	LifeHacker	Mashable
110.0	30.0	28.0	23.5	23.0

country with the most internet users

China

China dominates the world in Internet usage, with more than 642 million people—or about one-third of the country—browsing the World Wide Web under government censorship. The number of Internet users in China has tripled in the last five years. About 250 million Internet users browse from their cell phones. These phone-surfers account for much of the increase in Internet users. People spend an average of almost 20 hours a week online. Some Internet activities that are becoming increasingly popular in China include banking and booking travel.

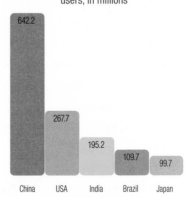

countries with the most internet users

users, in millions

China	USA	India	Brazil	Japan
642.2	267.7	195.2	109.7	99.7

bestselling cell phone brand

Samsung

Samsung commands more than 25 percent of the cell phone market, meaning that 1 in every 4 phones sold is made by that company. Samsung leads the smartphone market as well, with about 32 percent of all sales. In 2013, Samsung sold more than 319 million smartphones worldwide. One of Samsung's most popular phone brands is the Galaxy. There are five different types of these smartphones, and all are Android devices. The less-expensive models are in demand and sell very quickly in developing countries.

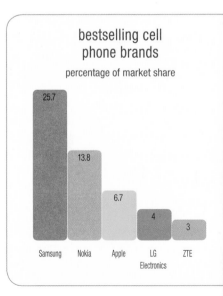

bestselling cell phone brands

percentage of market share

Samsung	Nokia	Apple	LG Electronics	ZTE
25.7	13.8	6.7	4	3

united states' bestselling smartphones

Android

The Android maintains the lead in the American smartphone race, with 52 percent of the market share. They are most popular with buyers ages 18 to 34, and men slightly outnumber women in ownership rates. On average, Android users have 22 apps. The top four apps on the Android are Google Maps, Facebook, the Weather Channel, and Pandora. And users remain loyal—more than 70 percent of current Android users intend to buy another when the time to upgrade comes. About 57 percent of US cell phone users now own a smartphone.

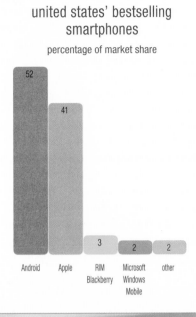

united states' bestselling smartphones
percentage of market share

Android	Apple	RIM Blackberry	Microsoft Windows Mobile	other
52	41	3	2	2

most popular mobile app

Facebook

Smartphone users check their Facebook app most, with 103.4 million unique users each month. Facebook also dominates a smartphone user's mobile time, accounting for 23 percent of the time the user is checking apps. That's more than the next six most popular apps combined. While browsing their Facebook apps, users can post and check status updates, share and view photos, and read and send private messages. Facebook has more than 1 billion users.

most popular mobile apps
average unique users, in millions

Facebook	Google Search	Google Play	YouTube	Google Maps
103.4	75.9	73.6	71.9	68.5

bestselling app type

Games

Games are the top app choice among smartphone users, with about 32 percent of users downloading them. Some of the bestselling iPhone games include Minecraft-Pocket Edition, Angry Birds Star Wars, and Temple Run: Oz. Some of the most popular Android games include Subway Surfers, Temple Run: 02, and Angry Birds Friends. More than 25 percent of adults download apps regularly, and the average user has about 18 of them. Mobil app sales made up about $27 billion in 2013, and the two largest app stores—Google and Apple—each have at least 800,000 apps each.

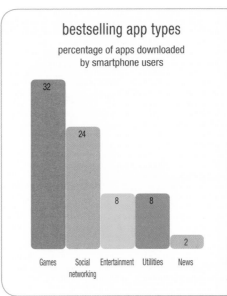

bestselling app types
percentage of apps downloaded by smartphone users

Games	Social networking	Entertainment	Utilities	News
32	24	8	8	2

bestselling e-book service

Amazon Kindle e-reader

Amazon's Kindle e-reader dominates the market, accounting for nearly half of all e-reader sales. The Kindle, which is a book-sized device onto which owners can download their favorite reading material, lets readers shop for and read books, magazines, and newspapers all in one spot. Some titles can be "loaned" to another Kindle user. The device also comes with a free electronic dictionary so users can look up unknown words as they read. The first Kindle was released in November 2007, but now comes in several models, including the original, Fire, and Paperwhite.

bestselling e-readers

percentage of the market

48.0	20.6	18.6	16.9	9.4
Amazon Kindle e-reader	Other	Pandigital	B&N Nook	Sony

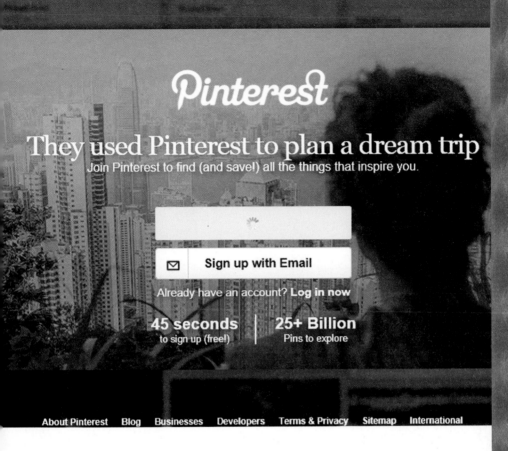

Pinterest

They used Pinterest to plan a dream trip
Join Pinterest to find (and save!) all the things that inspire you.

Sign up with Email

Already have an account? **Log in now**

45 seconds
to sign up (free!)

25+ Billion
Pins to explore

About Pinterest   Blog   Businesses   Developers   Terms & Privacy   Sitemap   International

fastest growing social media site

Pinterest

Pinterest—a website where users can post photos and ideas, and pin ones they like to their online bulletin boards—grew 80 percent between 2012 and 2013. Users can pin their interests to boards arranged according to themes, such as recipes, beauty, fashion, vacations, pets, and more. Once something is pinned to a board, the member has a link to the original site that the information came from and can access it at any time. Members can follow their friends' pins and boards as well. The site was launched in March 2010.

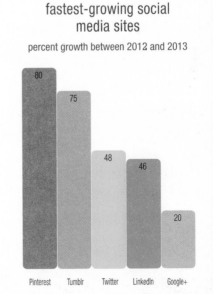

fastest-growing social media sites
percent growth between 2012 and 2013

Pinterest	Tumblr	Twitter	LinkedIn	Google+
80	75	48	46	20

largest cruise ships

Oasis of the Seas & Allure of the Seas

Royal Caribbean's sister cruise ships—*Oasis of the Seas* and *Allure of the Seas*—weigh in at 225,282 gross tons (228,897 t) each! These giant ships are more like floating cities with seven different themed neighborhoods: Central Park, Boardwalk, Royal Promenade, Pool and Sports Zone, Vitality at Sea Spa and Fitness Center, Entertainment Place, and Youth Zone. *Oasis of the Seas* and *Allure of the Seas* each feature 16 decks and include more than 20 eateries, 3 pools, a water park, and a zip-line ride. Both ships have 2,700 staterooms and can accommodate a whopping 5,400 guests.

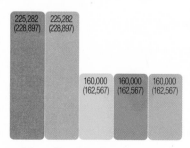

largest cruise ships
weight, in gross tons (tonnes)

Oasis of the Seas	Allure of the Seas	Independence of the Seas	Liberty of the Seas	Freedom of the Seas
225,282 (228,897)	225,282 (228,897)	160,000 (162,567)	160,000 (162,567)	160,000 (162,567)

Oasis of the Seas

fastest passenger train

CRH380AL

When China unveiled the CRH380AL commercial passenger train in 2010, it cruised into the record books with a top speed of 302 miles (486 km) per hour. The train reached its top speed in just 22 minutes. Its lightweight aluminum body and streamlined head help the CRH380AL travel that fast. The train's route connects Beijing and Shanghai, and reduced the average travel time from 10 hours to 4 hours. The train is part of China's $313 billion program to develop the world's most advanced train system by 2020.

fastest passenger trains

maximum speed, in miles (kilometers) per hour

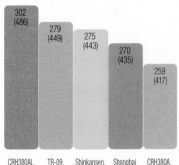

CRH380AL, China	TR-09, Germany	Shinkansen, Japan	Shanghai MagLev, China	CRH380A, China
302 (486)	279 (449)	275 (443)	270 (435)	259 (417)

33

biggest monster truck

Bigfoot 5

The Bigfoot 5 truly is a monster—it measures 15.4 feet (4.7 m) high! That's about three times the height of an average car. Bigfoot 5 has 10-foot (3 m) Firestone Tundra tires, each weighing 2,400 pounds (1,088 kg), giving the truck a total weight of about 38,000 pounds (17,236 kg). The giant wheels were from an arctic snow train operated in Alaska by the US Army in the 1950s. This modified 1996 Ford F250 pickup truck is owned by Bob Chandler of St. Louis, Missouri. The great weight of this monster truck makes it too large to race.

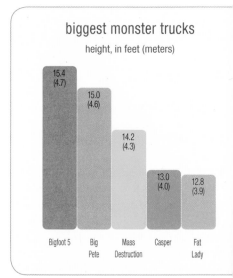

biggest monster trucks

height, in feet (meters)

15.4 (4.7)	15.0 (4.6)	14.2 (4.3)	13.0 (4.0)	12.8 (3.9)
Bigfoot 5	Big Pete	Mass Destruction	Casper	Fat Lady

smallest production car

Peel P50

The Peel P50 is the smallest production car ever made, measuring just 4.5 feet (1.4 m) long. That's not much longer than the average adult bicycle! The Peel P50 was originally produced in the Isle of Man between 1962 and 1965, and only 46 cars were made. However, the company began production again in 2012. The Peel P50 has three wheels, one door, one windshield wiper, and one headlight. The microcar weighs just 130 pounds (58.9 kg) and measures about 4 feet (1.2 m) tall. With its three-speed manual transmission, it can reach a top speed of 38 miles (61 km) an hour. It cannot, however, go in reverse.

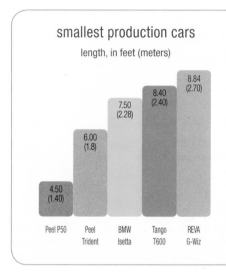

smallest production cars

length, in feet (meters)

Peel P50	Peel Trident	BMW Isetta	Tango T600	REVA G-Wiz
4.50 (1.40)	6.00 (1.8)	7.50 (2.28)	8.40 (2.40)	8.84 (2.70)

fastest land vehicle

Thrust SSC

The Thrust SSC, which stands for Supersonic Car, reached a speed of 763 miles (1,228 km) per hour on October 15, 1997. At that speed, a car could make it from San Francisco to New York City in less than four hours. The Thrust SSC is propelled by two jet engines capable of 110,000 horsepower. It has the same power as 1,000 Ford Escorts or 145 Formula One race cars. The Thrust SSC runs on jet fuel, using about 5 gallons (19 L) per second. It takes only approximately five seconds for this supersonic car to reach its top speed. It is 54 feet (16.5 m) long and weighs 7 tons (6.4 t).

fastest land vehicles

maximum speed, in miles (kilometers) per hour

Thrust SSC, 1997	Thrust 2, 1983	Blue Flame, 1970	Spirit of America, 1965	Green Monster, 1965
763 (1,228)	633 (1,019)	630 (1,014)	600 (966)	576 (927)

fastest production motorcycle

MTT Turbine Superbike Y2K

The MTT Turbine Superbike Y2K—the first turbine-powered, street-legal motorcycle—hits a top speed of 230 miles (370 km/h) per hour, or about 3.5 times the speed on an average highway. A Rolls-Royce Allison gas turbine engine powers the bike, and its aluminum-alloy frame and carbon-fiber fairings keep the weight down. The MTT Turbine Superbike also features a two-speed automatic transmission, Pirelli tires, and Brembo brakes, and comes in any color the buyer can imagine. The bike retails for about $175,000.

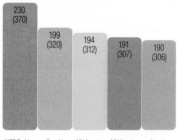

fastest production motorcycles

maximum speed, in miles (kilometers) per hour

MTT Turbine Superbike Y2K	Suzuki Hyabusa	MV Agusta F4 R312	MV Agusta F3 Tamburini	Ducati Desmosedici RR
230 (370)	199 (320)	194 (312)	191 (307)	190 (306)

fastest production car

Bugatti Veyron 16.4 Super Sport

With a top cruising speed of 268 miles (431 km) per hour, the Bugatti Veyron 16.4 Super Sport is the fastest production car in the world. It can cruise at more than four times the average speed limit on most highways! The Super Sport has a sleek, aerodynamic design that feeds air to the 16-cylinder engine from the roof, rather than just above the hood. The shell of the car is made of carbon-fiber composites to make the car lighter, while maintaining its safety. The Super Sport debuted at the Pebble Beach Concourse in August 2010.

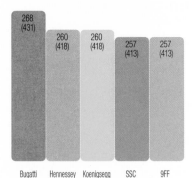

fastest production cars
maximum speed, in miles (kilometers) per hour

Bugatti Veyron 16.4 Super Sport	Hennessey Venom GT	Koenigsegg Agera R	SSC Ultimate Aero	9FF GT9-R
268 (431)	260 (418)	260 (418)	257 (413)	257 (413)

fastest helicopter

Eurocopter x3

The Eurocopter X3 can fly up to 302 miles (486 km) per hour. That's the same speed as the fastest train on Earth! The X3 uses three different rotating blades—one large blade on the roof, and two smaller blades on each side of the helicopter. It's powered by 2 Rolls-Royce Turbomeca RTM322 engines, and each engine can produce 2,270 horsepower. The aircraft can fly at about 12,500 feet (3810 m). Although it is still in the experimental stages, the X3 will probably be used for military missions as well as civilian search and rescue.

fastest helicopters

maximum speed, in miles (kilometers) per hour

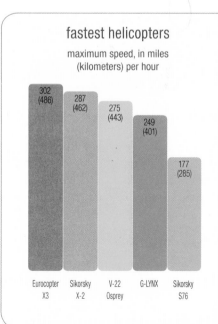

Eurocopter X3	Sikorsky X-2	V-22 Osprey	G-LYNX	Sikorsky S76
302 (486)	287 (462)	275 (443)	249 (401)	177 (285)

lightest jet

BD-5J Microjet

The BD-5J Microjet weighs only 358.8 pounds (162.7 kg), making it the lightest jet in the world. At only 12 feet (3.7 m) in length, it is one of the smallest as well. This tiny jet has a height of 5.6 feet (1.7 m) and a wingspan of 17 feet (5.2 m). The Microjet uses a TRS-18 turbojet engine. It can reach a top speed of 320 miles (514.9 km) per hour, but can carry only 32 gallons (121 L) of fuel at a time. A new BD-5J costs around $200,000. This high-tech gadget was flown by James Bond in the movie *Octopussy*, and it is also occasionally used by the US military.

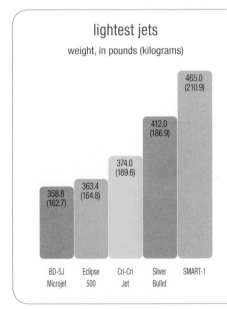

lightest jets
weight, in pounds (kilograms)

Jet	Weight
BD-5J Microjet	358.8 (162.7)
Eclipse 500	363.4 (164.8)
Cri-Cri Jet	374.0 (169.6)
Silver Bullet	412.0 (186.9)
SMART-1	465.0 (210.9)

fastest plane

X-43A

NASA's experimental X-43A plane reached a top speed of Mach 9.8—or more than nine times the speed of sound—on a test flight over the Pacific Ocean in November 2004. The X-43A was mounted on top of a Pegasus rocket booster and was carried into the sky by a B-52 aircraft. The booster was then fired, taking the X-43A about 110,000 feet (33,530 m) above the ground. The rocket was detached from the unmanned X-43A, and the plane flew unassisted for several minutes. At this rate of 7,459 miles (12,004 km) per hour, a plane could circle Earth in just over three and a half hours!

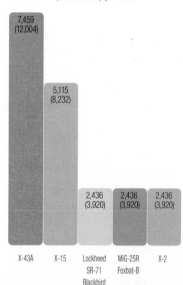

fastest planes

maximum speed, in miles (kilometers) per hour

Plane	Speed
X-43A	7,459 (12,004)
X-15	5,115 (8,232)
Lockheed SR-71 Blackbird	2,436 (3,920)
MiG-25R Foxbat-B	2,436 (3,920)
X-2	2,436 (3,920)

tallest roller coaster

Kingda Ka

Kingda Ka towers over Six Flags Great Adventure in Jackson, New Jersey, at a height of 456 feet (139 m). Its highest drop plummets riders down 418 feet (127 m). The steel coaster can reach a top speed of 128 miles (206 km) per hour in just 3.5 seconds, and it was the fastest coaster in the world when it opened in 2005. The entire 3,118-foot (950 m) ride is over in just 28 seconds. The hydraulic launch coaster is located in the Golden Kingdom section of the park. It can accommodate about 1,400 riders per hour.

tallest roller coasters
height, in feet (meters)

Kingda Ka, USA	Top Thrill Dragster, USA	Superman: Escape from Krypton, USA	Tower of Terror, Australia	Steel Dragon 2000, Japan
456 (139)	420 (128)	415 (126)	377 (115)	318 (97)

amusement park with the most rides

Cedar Point

Located in Sandusky, Ohio, Cedar Point offers park visitors 72 rides to enjoy. GateKeeper—one of the park's newest ride—is the fastest and longest-running winged roller coaster in the world. Top Thrill Dragster roller coaster is the second tallest in the world at 420 feet (128 m). And with 17 roller coasters, Cedar Point also has the most coasters of any theme park in the world. Over 53,963 feet (16,448 m) of coaster track—more than 10 miles (16.1 km)—run through the park. Cedar Point has been named Best Amusement Park in the World by *Amusement Today* for the past 16 years.

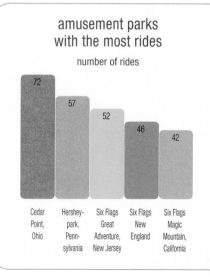

amusement parks
with the most rides

number of rides

Cedar Point, Ohio	Hershey-park, Penn-sylvania	Six Flags Great Adventure, New Jersey	Six Flags New England	Six Flags Magic Mountain, California
72	57	52	46	42

43

fastest roller coaster

Formula Rossa

The Formula Rossa coaster in the United Arab Emirates speeds past the competition with a top speed of 149 miles (240 km) per hour. Located at Ferrari World in Dubai, riders climb into the F1 race car cockpits and can experience what 4.8 g-force actually feels like. The coaster's hydraulic launch system rockets the coaster to its top speed in just 4.9 seconds. The track is about 1.4 miles (2.2 km) long, with the sharpest turn measuring 70 degrees.

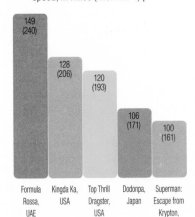

fastest roller coasters

speed, in miles (kilometers) per hour

Formula Rossa, UAE	Kingda Ka, USA	Top Thrill Dragster, USA	Dodonpa, Japan	Superman: Escape from Krypton, USA
149 (240)	128 (206)	120 (193)	106 (171)	100 (161)

city with the most skyscrapers

New York

New York City has the most skyscrapers in the world with 215 buildings that reach 500 feet (152 m) or higher. The three tallest buildings in the Big Apple are One World Trade Center at 1,776 feet (541 m), the Empire State Building at 1,250 feet (381 m), and the Bank of America Tower at 1,200 feet (366 m). One World Trade Center is the tallest building in the Western Hemisphere. The first skyscrapers popped up in New York City in the mid-1890s. With more than 22.1 million people currently living in the metropolitan area, architects have to continue building up instead of out.

cities with the most skyscrapers

number of skyscrapers

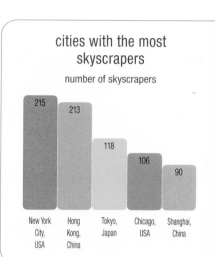

New York City, USA	Hong Kong, China	Tokyo, Japan	Chicago, USA	Shanghai, China
215	213	118	106	90

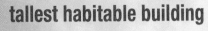

tallest habitable building
Burj Khalifa

Burj Khalifa in the United Arab Emirates towers 2,717 feet (828 m) above the ground. With more than 160 floors, the building cost about $4.1 billion to construct. Both a hotel and apartments are housed inside the luxury building, which covers 500 acres (202 ha). The building features high-speed elevators that travel at 40 miles (64 km) per hour. The tower supplies its occupants with about 250,000 gallons (66,043 l) of water a day, and delivers enough electricity to power 360,000 100-watt lightbulbs.

tallest habitable buildings
height, in feet (meters)

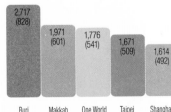

2,717 (828)	1,971 (601)	1,776 (541)	1,671 (509)	1,614 (492)
Burj Khalifa, UAE	Makkah Clock Royal Tower, Saudi Arabia	One World Trade Center, USA	Taipei 101, Taiwan	Shanghai World Financial Center, China

largest swimming pool

San Alfonso Del Mar

The gigantic swimming pool at the resort, in Chile, spreads over 19.7 acres (8 ha). The humongous pool is the equivalent to 6,000 standard swimming pools and holds 66 million gallons (250 million L) of water. In addition to swimming, guests can sail and scuba dive in the saltwater lagoon, which is surrounded by white sand beaches. And there's no diving for pennies here—the deep end measures 115 feet (35 m). The pool took five years to complete and first opened in December 2006. The project cost $2 billion, and it costs about $4 million annually to maintain.

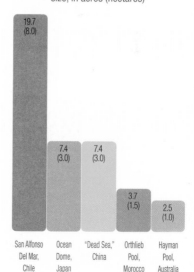

largest swimming pools
size, in acres (hectares)

San Alfonso Del Mar, Chile	Ocean Dome, Japan	"Dead Sea," China	Orthlieb Pool, Morocco	Hayman Pool, Australia
19.7 (8.0)	7.4 (3.0)	7.4 (3.0)	3.7 (1.5)	2.5 (1.0)

largest sports stadium

Rungrado May First Stadium

The Rungrado May First Stadium, also known as the May Day Stadium, can seat up to 150,000 people. The interior of the stadium covers 2.2 million square feet (204,386 sq m). Located in Pyongyang, North Korea, this venue is mostly used for soccer matches and other athletic contests. It is named after Rungra Island, on which the stadium is located, in the middle of the Taedong River. When it is not being used for sporting events, the stadium is used for a two-month gymnastics and artistic festival known as Arirang.

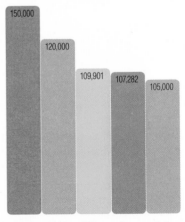

largest sports stadiums
number of seats

Rungrado May First Stadium, North Korea	Salt Lake Stadium, India	Michigan Stadium, USA	Beaver Stadium, USA	Estadio Azteca, Mexico
150,000	120,000	109,901	107,282	105,000

busiest airport

Hartsfield-Jackson Atlanta International Airport

The Hartsfield-Jackson Atlanta International Airport has about 94.4 million people land or depart from its gates each year. Approximately 2,500 planes depart and arrive at this airport every day. With parking lots, runways, maintenance facilities, and other buildings, the Hartsfield terminal complex covers about 130 acres (53 ha). Hartsfield-Jackson Atlanta International Airport has a north and a south terminal, an underground train, and seven concourses, with a total of 167 domestic and 40 international gates.

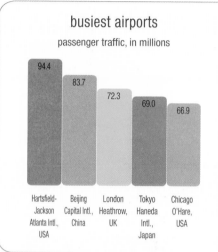

busiest airports
passenger traffic, in millions

- Hartsfield-Jackson Atlanta Intl., USA — 94.4
- Beijing Capital Intl., China — 83.7
- London Heathrow, UK — 72.3
- Tokyo Haneda Intl., Japan — 69.0
- Chicago O'Hare, USA — 66.9

49

country that produces the most cars

China

China leads the world in car production; it builds 16.6 million vehicles annually. Some of China's most popular car brands include Chery, Great Wall, Gely, and Chang'an. International brands with factories in China include Volkswagen, General Motors, and Honda. Most of the cars that are produced in China are also sold there. Approximately 1 million cars are exported annually. China's growth in the car production industry is fairly recent. Since the country joined the World Trade Organization in 2001, China's car production has grown by about 2.5 million vehicles annually.

countries that produce the most cars

number of cars produced annually, in millions

Country	Cars produced (millions)
China	16.6
Japan	7.8
Germany	5.4
USA	4.5
South Korea	4.1

greenest city

Vancouver

Vancouver, Canada, has been named the greenest city in the world for 2014 by GreenUpTown.com. Vancouver has been working very hard for this title, and assembled the GCAT (Greenest City Action Team) to help them form the Greenest Cities 2020 Action Plan. This plan was created by the businesses, government, and residents of Vancouver to improve their environment and set a green example for the rest of the world. They created this extensive plan in 2011 to cut carbon and waste production, and to nurture ecosystems. Some specific goals include creating 20,000 new green jobs, cutting carbon emissions by 33 percent, increasing use of renewable energy, and reducing waste by 40 percent.

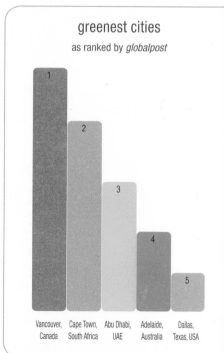

greenest cities
as ranked by *globalpost*

1	2	3	4	5
Vancouver, Canada	Cape Town, South Africa	Abu Dhabi, UAE	Adelaide, Australia	Dallas, Texas, USA

51

Money Records

Music Money Makers

Coachella is the most expensive music festival in the US, with three-day passes averaging about $933 for week one and $764 for week two. The show is held at the Empire Polo Club in Indio, California, and takes place during the second and third weekends of April. Some of the most popular artists performing in 2014 included Lorde, Muse, Arcade Fire, Pharrell, and Ellie Goulding.

First-Class Case

The world's most expensive iPad case hit the market in April 2014 at about $485,000. The top-of-the-line carrier is made of gold with specialized etchings, and features a sunburst design of diamonds and white gold. The case was created by Lucrezia Buccellati, who also created a matching iPhone case worth approximately $208,000.

Tweet Charity

With one single Twitter message, an anonymous benefactor donated 14 million Dogecoins—currency tradable online—worth about $11,000 to Doge4Water. This is the most money ever donated by a tweet. Doge4Water is a charity created by Dogecoin that builds new wells in Kenya to improve the quality of drinking water.

Racing into the Record Books

A 1954 Mercedes Benz W196 race car sold for $29.7 million in 2013, making it the most expensive automobile ever sold at auction. The car was part of a group of winning racers that dominated nine World Championship-qualifying Grand Prix races from 1954 to 1955. Classic cars were very popular at auctions in 2013, and collectively brought in more than $1 billion!

Rockers Rake It In

With tickets averaging $624 each when resold, the Rolling Stones 50th Anniversary Tour was the most expensive in 2013. The most expensive stop was on May 11 at the MGM Grand Garden Arena in Las Vegas, NV, where tickets averaged $1044. Band members include Mick Jagger, Keith Richards, Ronnie Wood, and Charlie Watts.

Pricey Pup

The most expensive piece of art sold by a living artist is *Balloon Dog (Orange)* by Jeff Koons, which brought in $58.4 million in November 2013. The stainless-steel sculpture is one in a series of five. The other four balloon dogs in the series were created in different colors—yellow, blue, magenta, and red. *Balloon Dog* stands 12 feet (3.7 m) high.

most expensive hotel

Royal Penthouse Suite

Guests better bring their wallets to the President Wilson Hotel in Geneva, Switzerland—the Royal Penthouse Suite costs $65,000 a night! That means a weeklong stay would total $455,000, which is almost twice the price of the average house in the US. The suite is reserved for heads of state and celebrities, and offers beautiful views of the Alps and Lake Geneva. The 18,082-square-foot (1,680 sq m) four-bedroom luxury suite has a private elevator and marble bathrooms. The state-of-the-art security system includes bulletproof doors and windows.

most expensive hotel
price per night, in US dollars

Hotel President Wilson, Switzerland	Raj Palace Hotel, India	Four Seasons Hotel, USA	Palms Fantasy Tower, USA	Hotel Martinez, France
65,000	45,000	41,000	40,000	37,000

most expensive comic book

Action Comics, No. 1

Action Comics, No. 1 sold for $2.1 million at auction in November 2011. This comic was published in April 1938 and introduced Superman to the world. Known as the world's first superhero comic, it featured the Man of Steel lifting up a car on its cover. It originally sold for 10 cents. Comic artists Jerry Siegel and Joe Shuster created the book and were paid $10 per page. About 200,000 copies were printed, but only about 100 survive today. Another copy of the same issue was auctioned off in March 2010, but sold for only $1.5 million because it was not in as good condition.

most expensive comic books

price, in US dollars

2.16M.	1.50M	1.38M	1.10M	1.00M
Action Comics, No. 1	Action Comics, No. 1	Detective Comics, No. 27	Amazing Fantasy, No. 15	Action Comics, No. 1

most expensive tv series ad slot in 2013

Sunday Night Football

For every 30-second commercial shown during *Sunday Night Football* in 2013, advertisers had to pay a whopping $593,700. That breaks down to $19,790 per second! That's also the same cost as 237 premium Super Bowl XLVIII tickets. *Sunday Night Football*—which was also the second-highest-rated show in 2013—is seen by about 21 million people each week, and advertisers want to capture their attention.

most expensive tv series ad slots in 2013

cost per commercial, in US dollars

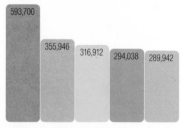

Sunday Night Football	American Idol	The Big Bang Theory	The Voice	American Idol Results
593,700	355,946	316,912	294,038	289,942

Cris Collinsworth and Al Michaels of *Sunday Night Football*

most valuable production car

Lamborghini Veneno Roadster

The Lamborghini Veneno costs a whopping $4.5 million—about 88 times the median income in the United States! The open-roof super sportscar boasts a 750-horsepower, V-12 engine and a 7-speed manual transmission. The Veneno can reach a top speed of 221 miles per hour (354 km/hr). It can accelerate from 0 to 60 in about 2.9 seconds. The car was created to celebrate Lamborghini's 50th anniversary. Only nine Veneno roadsters will be produced, and each will be metallic gray. The car was named after a famous Spanish fighting bull from the early 1900s.

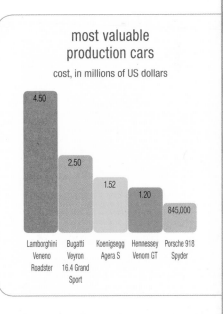

most valuable production cars

cost, in millions of US dollars

	Cost
Lamborghini Veneno Roadster	4.50
Bugatti Veyron 16.4 Grand Sport	2.50
Koenigsegg Agera S	1.52
Hennessey Venom GT	1.20
Porsche 918 Spyder	845,000

59

richest fictional character

Scrooge McDuck

If Disney's Scrooge McDuck were a real person, he would be worth an estimated $65.4 billion according to *Forbes Magazine*. This was determined by using information on the character's background. Scrooge made most of his money from mining and treasure hunting, and keeps his gold coins in the Duckburg money bin. McDuck was created in 1947 for a Disney cartoon. He is named after Ebenezer Scrooge, which is a character from the Charles Dickens novel *A Christmas Carol*. While he was originally not portrayed as a big spender, in later comics Scrooge McDuck is an adventurous explorer.

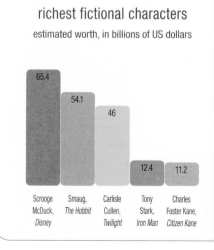

richest fictional characters

estimated worth, in billions of US dollars

Scrooge McDuck, Disney	Smaug, The Hobbit	Carlisle Cullen, Twilight	Tony Stark, Iron Man	Charles Foster Kane, Citizen Kane
65.4	54.1	46	12.4	11.2

world's most valuable brand

Apple

Apple—the computer company founded in 1976—is worth a staggering $104.3 billion. That's enough money to give every person living in the company's home state of California about $2,736. The company has sold more than 72 million modern Macs to date, and nearly 1 million people visit its more than 400 retail stores in 14 countries daily. Apple has also sold more than 700 million iPads, iPhones, and iPod-touches. About 900,000 iOS apps are available in the App Store. There are 300 million iCloud users across the globe, and this service has handled about 7.4 trillion push messages since it began.

world's most valuable brands

brand value, in billions of US dollars

Apple	Microsoft	Coca-Cola	IBM	Google
104.3	56.7	54.9	50.7	47.3

most valuable football team

Dallas Cowboys

Worth $2.3 billion, the Dallas Cowboys are the most valuable team in the National Football League for the seventh year in a row. In addition to ticket sales, the Cowboys have several side businesses that bring in the cash. In 2008, they launched Legends Hospitality Management, a company that consults with other team owners to maximize earnings. They also started Silver Star Merchandising to make and distribute team apparel. Cowboys Stadium has 320 suites and 15,000 club seats, and generates $500 million in revenue annually. The team and its loyal fans have enjoyed 21 division championships, 10 conference championships, and 5 Super Bowl championships since the franchise began in 1960.

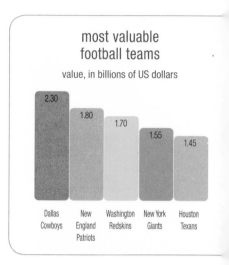

most valuable football teams

value, in billions of US dollars

Dallas Cowboys	New England Patriots	Washington Redskins	New York Giants	Houston Texans
2.30	1.80	1.70	1.55	1.45

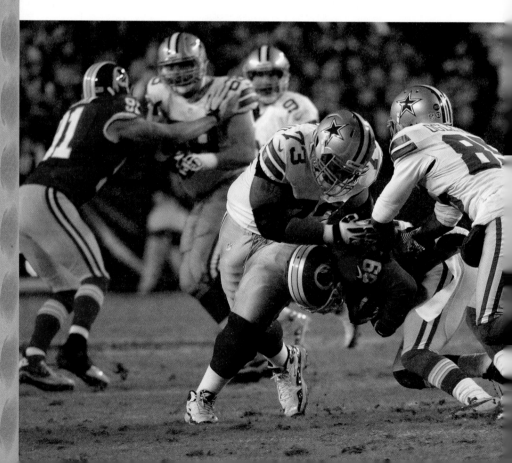

most valuable hockey team

Toronto Maple Leafs

The Toronto Maple Leafs are worth $1.15 billion, which is more than $400 million more than the average pro hockey team's value. The team's top ranking is largely due to strong ticket sales and television deals. Although Toronto won 13 Stanley Cups between 1917 and 1967, they have not won a cup in 46 years, which is the longest losing streak in the league. Toronto was one of the six teams that formed the National Hockey League in 1917. Their home arena is called Air Canada Centre.

most valuable hockey teams

value, in billions and millions of US dollars

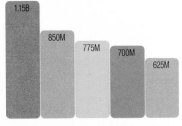

1.15B	850M	775M	700M	625M
Toronto Maple Leafs	New York Rangers	Montreal Canadiens	Detroit Red Wings	Boston Bruins

most valuable soccer team

Real Madrid

Spain's Real Madrid is valued at $3.3 billion. The team is also known as Los Merengues or Los Blancos (for their white uniforms). During the 2011–2012 season, Real Madrid won the La Liga league. This was the club's thirty-second win—a La Liga record. In 2014, Real Madrid finished the season poorly and placed third. The team has also won 9 European Cup/UEFA Championship League titles. The club has been home to some of the world's best-known players, including Cristiano Ronaldo and Raúl. Real Madrid was founded in 1902 and plays in the 85,454-seat Estadio Santiago Bernabeu.

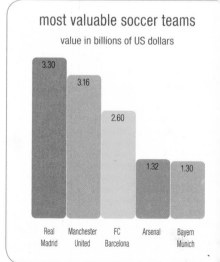

most valuable soccer teams
value in billions of US dollars

Real Madrid	Manchester United	FC Barcelona	Arsenal	Bayern Munich
3.30	3.16	2.60	1.32	1.30

athletes with the highest endorsement deals

Roger Federer & Tiger Woods

Tennis champ Roger Federer and golfing great Tiger Woods both earn about $65 million each year for endorsing all types of products. Federer—who has been ranked number one for more than 300 weeks during his ongoing career—pitches products for Nike, Gillette, Wilson, and Möet & Chandon. He also holds endorsements deals with companies based in his native country of Switzerland, including Rolex, Credit Suisse, and Lindt. Woods, who has been named PGA Player of the year a record 11 times, has endorsement deals with Nike, Rolex, Fuse Science, Upper Deck, and Kowa.

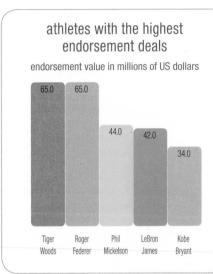

athletes with the highest endorsement deals

endorsement value in millions of US dollars

Tiger Woods	Roger Federer	Phil Mickelson	LeBron James	Kobe Bryant
65.0	65.0	44.0	42.0	34.0

Roger Federer

65

united states' bestselling automobiles

Ford F-Series

Ford sold 763,402 F-Series trucks during 2013. The F-Series originated in 1948, when the F-1 (half ton), the F-2 (three-quarter ton), and the F-3 (Heavy Duty) were introduced. Since then, many modifications and new editions have been introduced, including the F-150. The modern F-150 sports a V-6 or V-8 engine and the option of a regular, extended, or crew cab. The bed size ranges from 5.5 feet (1.6 m) to 8 feet (2.4 km). The Platinum F-150—the top-of-the-line version—features platinum chrome wheels, a fancy grille design, leather upholstery, and heated seats.

united states' bestselling automobiles

number of automobiles sold in 2013

763,402	480,414	408,484	366,673	355,673
Ford F-150	Chevrolet Silverado	Toyota Camry	Honda Accord	Ram Pickup

largest global retailer

Walmart

Megadiscount retail chain Walmart had more than $469 billion in sales during 2013. Walmart serves more than 245 million customers each week at its more than 11,000 stores. Located in 27 countries, the company employs more than 1.4 million people in the United States and another 800,000 worldwide. This makes Walmart one of the largest private employers in North America. Walmart is currently ranked number one on the *Fortune 500* list of most profitable companies.

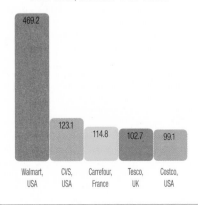

largest global retailers
2013 sales, in billions of US dollars

Walmart, USA	CVS, USA	Carrefour, France	Tesco, UK	Costco, USA
469.2	123.1	114.8	102.7	99.1

largest global food franchise

Subway

There are 41,176 Subway restaurants located throughout the world. There are 26,438 franchises in the United States, and another 14,738 international locations. Subway, which is owned by Doctor's Associates, Inc., had global sales totaling $18.1 billion in 2013. They had a brand value of $5.7 billion. The sandwich company was started by Fred DeLuca in 1965, and began franchising in 1974. Start-up fees run between $84,000 and $258,000, and 100 percent of the company is franchised. About 65 percent of franchisees own more than one location.

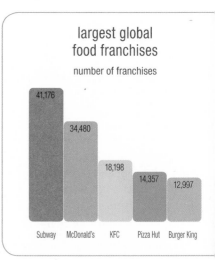

largest global food franchises
number of franchises

Subway	McDonald's	KFC	Pizza Hut	Burger King
41,176	34,480	18,198	14,357	12,997

largest retail franchise

7-Eleven

There are 50,460 7-Eleven convenience stores located around the world. Out of these, there are 8,144 locations in the United States and 42,316 locations internationally. The store chain is ranked number two on the *Forbes* Top 20 Franchises for the Buck list, meaning that investors have a very good chance of making a profit on their stores. The stores sell about 320 baked goods every minute, 13 million Slurpee beverages each month, and more than 100 milllion hot dogs each year. Approximately 25 percent of Americans live within a mile (1.6 km) of a 7-Eleven store.

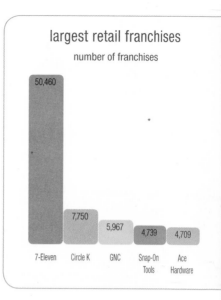

largest retail franchises
number of franchises

7-Eleven	50,460	
Circle K	7,750	
GNC	5,967	
Snap-On Tools	4,739	
Ace Hardware	4,709	

Pop Culture Records

television
movies
music
theater

Real-Time Sales

Reality TV shows had a huge impact on music downloads in 2013. After *The Voice* contestant James Wolpert sang Jack White's "Love Interruption," downloads of the original jumped 2,218 percent! When *The X Factor*'s Rion Page sang "Blown Away" by Carrie Underwood, downloads of that song shot up 1,902 percent.

Tune In and Tweet Often

Music, television, and tweeting all tie together. About 10 million viewers tuned in for the 2013 MTV Video Music Awards, and One Direction's Harry Styles's "VMA" tweet was retweeted more than 35 million times. The Billboard Music Awards had an audience of almost 9.5 million, and #Prince was included in 12,000 tweets, while #miguel was tweeted 19,000 times.

The Academy's Audience

Since the Academy Awards began in 1929, they have given out more than 280 statuettes. About 700 million people watch the event annually. Some 75 photographers are there to capture the excitement, along with 380 members of the press. Celebrities will walk down a 500-foot (152-m) long red carpet, and take home a goody bag worth at least $55,000.

Catch-Up by Country

After spending a few decades frozen in ice, the "catch-up" list of recent events that Captain America carries with him changes according to where the movie is playing. In the US, it includes *Star Wars*, *I Love Lucy*, and Steve Jobs among other things. The UK version adds the Beatles and Sean Connery. The French version includes Daft Punk, while the German version mentions the rise and fall of the Berlin Wall.

One Hot Role

Dane DeHaan, who plays the Green Goblin in *Amazing Spider-Man 2*, sweated off 7 pounds (3 kg) in just 2 days while wearing the 50-pound (22.6 kg) goblin costume and filming under intense lights on the closed soundstage. Producers tried pumping ice water into the costume, but it quickly turned to steam. They eventually fitted him with a cooling vest that hooked up to an ice water tank between scenes.

Creative Creatures

The creatures created for *The Lion King* on Broadway are truly works of wonder. More than 17,000 hours were spent completing the animal characters and masks. Over 750 pounds (340 kg) of silicone rubber were used to make the masks. The tallest animals, the giraffes, are 14 feet (4.2 m) and actors walk on stilts while inside.

It Pays to Be a Pirate

With production costs of more than $410 million, *Pirates of the Caribbean: On Stranger Tides* is the most expensive movie ever made. Johnny Depp, who starred as Captain Jack Sparrow, earned about $55 million for his role in the fourth installment in the series. The movie went on to earn more than $1.04 billion worldwide.

highest-paid tv actress

Mariska Hargitay

Law & Order: Special Victims Unit actress Mariska Hargitay earns $500,000 per episode for her role as Detective Olivia Benson. Since the NBC crime drama—also known simply as *SVU*—began in 1999, Hargitay has won an Emmy and a Golden Globe for her performance. The series focuses on the 16th Precinct of the New York Police Department, and follows the detectives and lawyers from when the crime is committed to how it plays out in the courtroom. The show is a spinoff of the original *Law & Order* series, and was the second in the franchise.

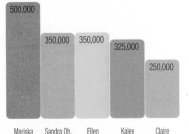

highest-paid tv actresses

salary per episode, 2013–2014 season in US dollars

500,000	350,000	350,000	325,000	250,000
Mariska Hargitay, *Law & Order SVU*	Sandra Oh, *Grey's Anatomy*	Ellen Pompeo, *Grey's Anatomy*	Kaley Cuoco, *The Big Bang Theory*	Claire Danes, *Homeland*

tv show with the most emmy awards

Saturday Night Live

The comedy sketch show *Saturday Night Live* has earned 40 Emmy Awards since it picked up its first four statues in 1976. Some of the categories that *SNL* has won awards for include Outstanding Variety, Music, or Comedy Series, Outstanding Guest Actor in a Comedy Series, Outstanding Original Music and Lyrics, and Outstanding Writing for a Variety, Musical, or Comedy Program. The show has launched the careers of many comedians that went on to be big stars, such as Chevy Chase, Bill Murray, Dana Carvey, Adam Sandler, Mike Myers, Tina Fey, and Andy Samberg.

tv shows with the most emmy awards
emmys won

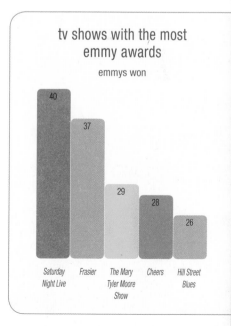

	emmys won
Saturday Night Live	40
Frasier	37
The Mary Tyler Moore Show	29
Cheers	28
Hill Street Blues	26

tv show with the most consecutive emmy awards

The Daily Show with Jon Stewart

The Daily Show with Jon Stewart has won an Emmy Award for Outstanding Variety, Music, or Comedy series for ten consecutive seasons between 2003 and 2012. In total, the show has received 27 Emmy nominations, and has won 18 of them. Although it is considered a fake news show, the program often uses actual recent news stories and delivers them with a funny or sarcastic spin. The show began in 1996, and it is the longest-running program on Comedy Central. *The Daily Show* was hosted by Craig Kilborn until 1998, when Kilborn was replaced by Stewart.

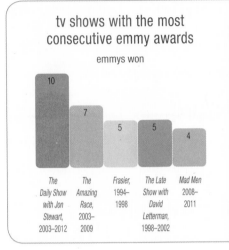

tv shows with the most consecutive emmy awards

emmys won

10	7	5	5	4
The Daily Show with Jon Stewart, 2003–2012	The Amazing Race, 2003–2009	Frasier, 1994–1998	The Late Show with David Letterman, 1998–2002	Mad Men 2008–2011

most popular tv show

NCIS

The CBS drama *NCIS* draws in an average of 21.6 million viewers each week. Every Tuesday, fans tune in to watch the members of the Naval Criminal Investigative Service solve crimes and restore justice. The team, which is led by Leroy Jethro Gibbs (Mark Harmon), is made up of Tony DiNozzo (Michael Weatherly), Timothy McGee (Sean Murray), Eleanor Bishop (Emily Wickersham), and Abby Sciuto (Pauley Perrette). The show debuted in 2003 and has produced more than 250 episodes. *NCIS* has been nominated for three Emmy Awards and six People's Choice Awards.

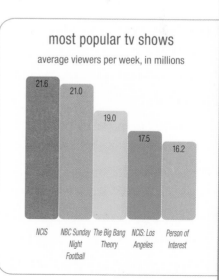

most popular tv shows
average viewers per week, in millions

NCIS	NBC Sunday Night Football	The Big Bang Theory	NCIS: Los Angeles	Person of Interest
21.6	21.0	19.0	17.5	16.2

celebrities with the most kids' choice awards

Adam Sandler

Kids love funny actors! With their votes, Adam Sandler has won 10 Nickelodeon Kids' Choice Awards since the show began in 1988. Sandler's awards include Favorite Movie Actor (1999, 2000, 2003, 2005, 2007, 2012, 2014), Favorite Voice From an Animated Movie (2003, 2013), and a Wannabe Award (2004). Some of Sandler's most popular recent movies include *Bedtime Stories* (2008), *Hotel Transylvania* (2012), *Grown Ups* (2010), and *Click* (2006). In addition to his Kid's Choice Awards, Sandler has also won two Teen Choice Awards, three People's Choice Awards, and five MTV Movie Awards.

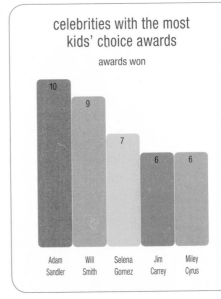

celebrities with the most
kids' choice awards
awards won

Adam Sandler	Will Smith	Selena Gomez	Jim Carrey	Miley Cyrus
10	9	7	6	6

highest-paid tv actor

Ashton Kutcher

Ashton Kutcher earns about $34,000 a minute for his role as Walden Schmidt—a brokenhearted millionaire—on *Two and a Half Men*. Kutcher debuted on the hit CBS comedy in September 2011 to replace Charlie Sheen. More than 27.7 million people tuned in to see his first episode— the largest audience in the show's history. Before joining *Two and a Half Men*, Kutcher starred in Fox's *That '70s Show*, and several movies, including *Dude, Where's My Car?*, *The Butterfly Effect*, and *What Happens in Vegas*. He also produced a reality show, *Punk'd*, for MTV.

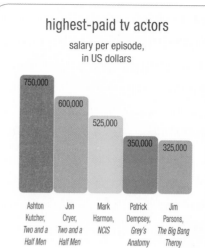

highest-paid tv actors

salary per episode, in US dollars

Ashton Kutcher, Two and a Half Men	Jon Cryer, Two and a Half Men	Mark Harmon, NCIS	Patrick Dempsey, Grey's Anatomy	Jim Parsons, The Big Bang Theroy
750,000	600,000	525,000	350,000	325,000

highest-paid celebrity couple
Jay-Z & Beyoncé

Powerhouse performers Jay-Z and Beyoncé earned $95 million in 2013. Beyonce contribution came partly from her Mrs. Carter world tour, which grossed more than $188 million worldwide. Beyonce also has several side ventures that brings in extra cash, including an endorsement deal with Pepsi and her own line of perfume. Jay-Z's income comes mainly from the album sales of *Watch the Throne*, which went platinum. His tour by the same name brought in about $1.4 million a night in the United States. Jay-Z is also launching his own sports agency— Roc Nation Sports—and his clients include Kevin Durant and Victor Cruz.

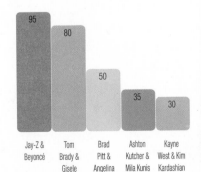

highest-paid celebrity couples

combined income in 2013,
in millions of US dollars

Jay-Z & Beyoncé	Tom Brady & Gisele Bündchen	Brad Pitt & Angelina Jolie	Ashton Kutcher & Mila Kunis	Kayne West & Kim Kardashian
95	80	50	35	30

highest-paid producer

Steven Spielberg

Legendary producer Steven Spielberg earned $100 million in 2013. Although Spielberg is best known for his films, he spent much of the year producing the television series *Under the Dome, Falling Skies,* and *Smash. Under the Dome* is a drama that follows the lives of people in a small town that is trapped under an invisible force field. The sci-fi thriller *Falling Skies* follows survivors of an alien attack. And *Smash* is a drama that centers on the cast of a Broadway musical about Marilyn Monroe. Spielberg also spent the year producing several films including *Transformers: Age of Extinction* (2014) and *The Hundred-Foot Journey* (2014).

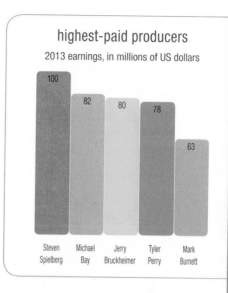

highest-paid producers
2013 earnings, in millions of US dollars

Steven Spielberg	Michael Bay	Jerry Bruckheimer	Tyler Perry	Mark Burnett
100	82	80	78	63

actor with the lowest returns per salary dollar

Adam Sandler

For every dollar that Adam Sandler gets paid, his movies bring in just $3.40. Sandler has had a tough few years at the box office as a leading man, bringing his career earning average way down. *That's My Boy* (2012), in which Sandler starred as Donny, had a production budget of $67 million, but earned just $58 million worldwide. During his career, Sandler has starred in 24 movies, and his box office average earnings are $77.5 million per film. While that may not sound too low, Sandler usually commands about $20 million per role.

actors with the lowest returns per salary dollar

return for every dollar paid, in US dollars

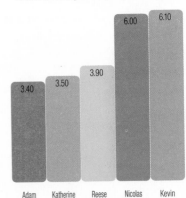

Adam Sandler	Katherine Heigl	Reese Witherspoon	Nicolas Cage	Kevin James
3.40	3.50	3.90	6.00	6.10

actors with the highest returns per salary dollar

Emma Stone

For every dollar that actress Emma Stone is paid, her movies generate $80.70 in box office earnings. Through 2013, Stone starred in six films, and each earned an average of $191.5 million. Her most successful movie was *The Amazing Spider-Man* (2012) in which she played Gwen Stacy. It earned $757 million worldwide. She also lent her voice to Eep in *The Croods* (2013), which earned $573 million, and played Skeeter in *The Help* (2011), which earned $213 million. Stone will reprise her role as Gwen in *The Amazing Spider-Man 2* in 2014. Stone has won two MTV Movie Awards, three Teen Choice Awards, and one People's Choice Award.

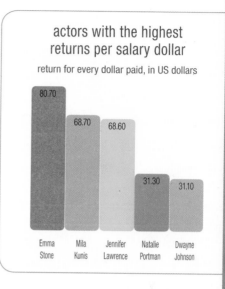

actors with the highest returns per salary dollar

return for every dollar paid, in US dollars

Emma Stone	Mila Kunis	Jennifer Lawrence	Natalie Portman	Dwayne Johnson
80.70	68.70	68.60	31.30	31.10

actress with the most oscar nominations

Meryl Streep

Meryl Streep is the most-nominated actress in the history of the Academy Awards, with 18 chances to win a statue. Her first nomination came in 1979 for *The Deer Hunter*, and was followed by *Kramer vs. Kramer* (1980), *The French Lieutenant's Woman* (1981), *Sophie's Choice* (1982), *Silkwood* (1983), *Out of Africa* (1985), *Ironweed* (1987), *A Cry in the Dark* (1988), *Postcards From the Edge* (1990), *The Bridges of Madison County* (1995), *One True Thing* (1998), *Music of the Heart* (1999), *Adaptation* (2002), *The Devil Wears Prada* (2006), *Doubt* (2008), *Julie and Julia* (2009), *The Iron Lady* (2012), and *August: Osage County* (2013). Streep won her first Academy Award for *Kramer vs. Kramer,* her second for *Sophie's Choice*, and a third for *The Iron Lady*.

actresses with the most oscar nominations

oscar nominations

Meryl Streep	Katharine Hepburn	Bette Davis	Geraldine Page	Judi Dench
18	12	10	8	7

actor with the most oscar nominations

Jack Nicholson

Jack Nicholson has been nominated for a record 12 Oscars during his distinguished career. He is one of only three men to have been nominated for an acting Academy Award at least once every decade for five decades. He was nominated for eight Best Actor awards for his roles in *Five Easy Pieces* (1970), *The Last Detail* (1973), *Chinatown* (1974), *One Flew Over the Cuckoo's Nest* (1975), *Prizzi's Honor* (1985), *Ironweed* (1987), *As Good as It Gets* (1997), and *About Schmidt* (2002). He was nominated for Best Supporting Actor for *Easy Rider* (1969), *Reds* (1981), *Terms of Endearment* (1983), and *A Few Good Men* (1992). Nicholson picked up statues for *One Flew Over the Cuckoo's Nest*, *Terms of Endearment*, and *As Good as It Gets*.

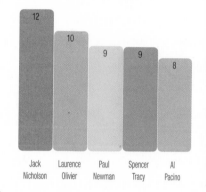

actors with the most oscar nominations

oscar nominations

Jack Nicholson	Laurence Olivier	Paul Newman	Spencer Tracy	Al Pacino
12	10	9	9	8

actor with the most mtv movie awards

Jim Carrey

Jim Carrey has won 11 MTV Movie Awards since the television station began awarding them in 1992. He has won the award for Best Comedic Performance five times, for his roles in *Dumb & Dumber* (1995), *Ace Ventura II: When Nature Calls* (1996), *The Cable Guy* (1997), *Liar Liar* (1998), and *Yes Man* (2009). Carrey won the award for Best Male Performance twice, for *Ace Ventura II: When Nature Calls* and *The Truman Show* (1999). He also won awards for Best Kiss for *Dumb & Dumber*, Best Villain for *The Cable Guy*, and the MTV Generation Award in 2006.

actors with the most mtv movie awards

awards won

Jim Carrey	Robert Pattinson	Mike Myers	Adam Sandler	Johnny Depp
11	10	7	6	5

actress with the most mtv movie awards

Kristen Stewart

Kristen Stewart, who rose to fame playing Bella Swan in the *Twilight* saga, won seven MTV Movie Awards for her role. She picked up her first two awards—Best Female Performance and Best Kiss—in 2009 for *Twilight*. She shared the Best Kiss award with costar Robert Pattinson. A year later, she picked up the same two awards for *New Moon*. In 2011, Stewart nabbed the same two again for *Eclipse*. Stewart's most recent award win came in 2012, when she once again shared the Best Kiss award with Robert Pattinson for the 2011 *Twilight* film, *Breaking Dawn: Part One*.

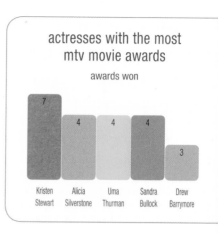

actresses with the most mtv movie awards

awards won

Kristen Stewart	Alicia Silverstone	Uma Thurman	Sandra Bullock	Drew Barrymore
7	4	4	4	3

movies with the most oscars

Ben-Hur, Titanic, and The Lord of the Rings: The Return of the King

The only three films in Hollywood history to win 11 Academy Awards are *Ben-Hur*, *Titanic*, and *The Lord of the Rings: The Return of the King*. Some of the Oscar wins for *Ben-Hur*—a biblical epic based on an 1880 novel by General Lew Wallace—include Best Actor (Charlton Heston) and Director (William Wyler). Some of *Titanic*'s Oscars include Best Cinematography, Visual Effects, and Costume Design. *The Lord of the Rings: The Return of the King* is the final film in the epic trilogy based on the works of J.R.R. Tolkien. With 11 awards, it is the most successful movie in Academy Awards history because it won every category in which it was nominated. Some of these wins include Best Picture, Director (Peter Jackson), and Costume Design.

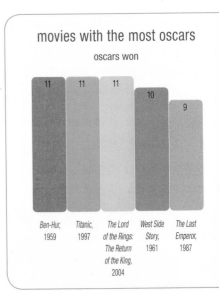

movies with the most oscars
oscars won

Ben-Hur, 1959	Titanic, 1997	The Lord of the Rings: The Return of the King, 2004	West Side Story, 1961	The Last Emperor, 1987
11	11	11	10	9

Presenters and the cast of *The Lord of the Rings* (Peter Jackson in front)

actor with the highest career box-office gross

Frank Welker

Frank Welker's movies have a combined total gross of $6.60 billion. Although movie fans might not recognize Welker's name or face, they would probably recognize many of his voices. Welker is a voice actor, and has worked on more than 90 movies in the last 25 years. Some of his most famous voices include Megatron, Curious George, and Scooby-Doo. Welker's most profitable movies include *How the Grinch Stole Christmas*, *Godzilla*, and *101 Dalmatians*.

actors with the highest career box-office gross

total gross, in billions of US dollars*

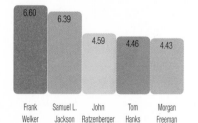

Frank Welker	Samuel L. Jackson	John Ratzenberger	Tom Hanks	Morgan Freeman
6.60	6.39	4.59	4.46	4.43

*As of March 2014

top-grossing animated movie

Frozen

Disney's animated adventure *Frozen* has earned more than $1 billion worldwide since it opened in November 2013. It's one of the ten highest-grossing films of all time. The story centers on sisters Elsa and Anna, and how Elsa's special powers keep the sisters apart. Anna—voiced by Kristen Bell—is a free spirit, while Elsa—voiced by Idina Menzel—is a bit more reserved. Together with ice salesman Kristoff (Jonathan Groff), Olaf the snowman (Josh Gad), and a helpful reindeer named Sven, the sisters battle to overcome their differences and be a family again. The movie won Academy Awards for Best Animated Feature and Best Original Song.

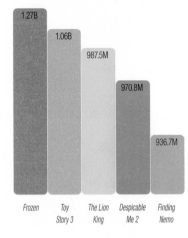

top-grossing animated movies

worldwide gross earnings, in millions of US dollars*

Frozen	Toy Story 3	The Lion King	Despicable Me 2	Finding Nemo
1.27B	1.06B	987.5M	970.8M	936.7M

*As of July 2014

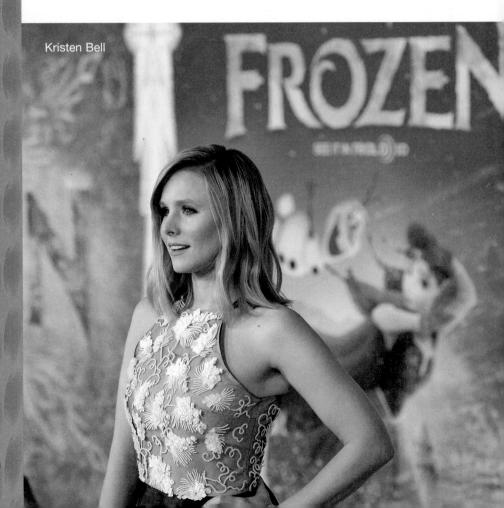

Kristen Bell

movie with the most successful domestic opening weekend

Marvel's The Avengers

On May 4, 2012, people flocked to theaters and spent more than $207 million to see *Marvel's The Avengers*. The movie has a worldwide gross of $1.51 billion, and is the third-highest-grossing movie of all time. DVD sales added another $68 million. The movie tells the story of the comic book superheroes including Iron Man, Captain America, the Hulk, and Thor, and its stars include Robert Downey Jr., Samuel L. Jackson, Mark Ruffalo, Scarlett Johansson, and Chris Hemsworth. It was directed by Joss Whedon and released by Walt Disney Studios. *Marvel's The Avengers* had a budget of about $220 million.

movies with the most successful domestic opening weekend

weekend earnings, in millions of US dollars

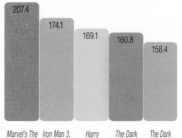

Marvel's The Avengers, 5/4/12	Iron Man 3, 5/3/13	Harry Potter and the Deathly Hallows: Part 2, 7/15/11	The Dark Knight Rises, 7/20/12	The Dark Knight, 7/18/08
207.4	174.1	169.1	160.8	158.4

top-grossing movie

Avatar

Avatar, James Cameron's science-fiction epic, was released in December 2009 and grossed more than $2.78 billion worldwide in less than two months. Starring Sigourney Weaver, Sam Worthington, and Zoe Saldana, *Avatar* cost more than $230 million to make. Cameron began working on the film in 1994, and it was eventually filmed in 3-D, with special cameras made just for the movie. Due to *Avatar*'s overwhelming success, Cameron is already planning two sequels.

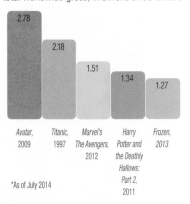

top-grossing movies

total worldwide gross, in billions of US dollars*

2.78	2.18	1.51	1.34	1.27
Avatar, 2009	Titanic, 1997	Marvel's The Avengers, 2012	Harry Potter and the Deathly Hallows: Part 2, 2011	Frozen, 2013

*As of July 2014

most successful movie franchise

Harry Potter

The eight movies in the Harry Potter franchise have collectively earned $7.7 billion. The series, which began in November 2001, is based on the bestselling books by J.K. Rowling. They chronicle the adventures of a young wizard—Harry Potter—as he grows up and learns of the great power he possesses. The highest-grossing movie in the franchise is the last one—*Harry Potter and the Deathly Hallows: Part 2*—which earned $1.3 billion worldwide. The leads of the movie, including Daniel Radcliffe, Rupert Grint, and Emma Watson, have become some of the highest-paid young stars in Hollywood.

most successful movie franchises

total worldwide gross,
in billions of US dollars*

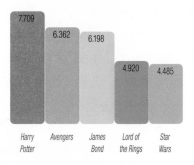

Harry Potter	Avengers	James Bond	Lord of the Rings	Star Wars
7.709	6.362	6.198	4.920	4.485

*As of July 2014

93

top-earning actor

Robert Downey Jr.

Robert Downey Jr. raked in $75 million in 2013, mostly due to the great success of *Iron Man 3*. In the movie, Downey plays Tony Stark, also known as the superhero Iron Man. It was released in May 2013 and earned $1.21 billion worldwide. The prequel, *Marvel's The Avengers*, was released a year earlier and brought in $1.5 billion across the globe. Downey also has another successful movie franchise—*Sherlock Holmes*. Between 2009 and 2011, the actor completed two of these films, which earned a combined total of $1 billion worldwide. Downey also picked up a Golden Globe for Best Actor in 2009 for his role as Holmes.

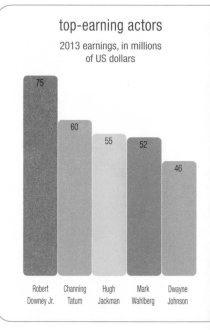

top-earning actors

2013 earnings, in millions of US dollars

Robert Downey Jr.	Channing Tatum	Hugh Jackman	Mark Wahlberg	Dwayne Johnson
75	60	55	52	46

top-earning actress
Angelina Jolie

During 2013, Angelina Jolie brought in $33 million. Although she has not had a film at the box office during the year, she collected royalties and income from past projects. Some of her recent projects include voicing the Tigress in *Kung Fu Panda 2* (2011), which earned $664 million worldwide, and playing Elise Ward in *The Tourist* (2010), which grossed $278 million across the globe. Jolie also made her directorial debut in 2011 with the movie *In the Land of Blood and Honey*, which earned her a Golden Globe nomination. Jolie returned to acting with the title role in Disney's *Maleficent* (2014).

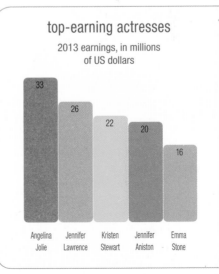

top-earning actresses

2013 earnings, in millions of US dollars

Angelina Jolie	Jennifer Lawrence	Kristen Stewart	Jennifer Aniston	Emma Stone
33	26	22	20	16

actor with the largest paycheck for a single character

Tom Cruise

For playing the role of Agent Ethan Hunt in all four *Mission Impossible* movies, Tom Cruise earned a whopping $290 million. Since Cruise's own film studio produced all of the movies in the franchise, he earned between $70 million to $75 million for each one. The movies, which were filmed between 1996 and 2011, also did extremely well at the box office, earning a combined $2.09 billion worldwide. *Mission Impossible 5* is due to hit theaters in December 2015. The movies have earned Cruise three Kids' Choice Awards and three Teen Choice Award nominations, as well as one MTV Movie Award.

actors with the largest paycheck for a single character

total earnings, in millions of US dollars

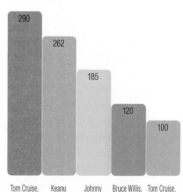

Tom Cruise, *Mission Impossible* franchise	Keanu Reeves, *The Matrix* franchise	Johnny Depp, *Pirates of the Caribbean* franchise	Bruce Willis, *The Sixth Sense*	Tom Cruise, *War of the Worlds*
290	262	185	120	100

The Hunger Games: Catching Fire

Catching Fire—the second installment in *The Hunger Games* franchise—topped box office receipts in 2013 with $424.3 million in the US and $433.0 internationally. The movie stars Jennifer Lawrence as Katniss Everdeen, Josh Hutcherson as Peeta Mellark, and Liam Hemsworth as Gale Hawthorne. The plot follows the second book of Suzanne Collin's trilogy. Katniss and Peeta return to Panem as the winners of the Hunger Games and embark on their Victory Tour. The film cost about $130 million to produce, and was released by Lionsgate in November 2013.

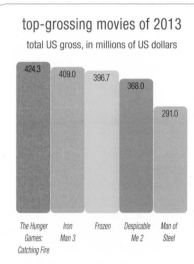

top-grossing movies of 2013
total US gross, in millions of US dollars

The Hunger Games: Catching Fire	Iron Man 3	Frozen	Despicable Me 2	Man of Steel
424.3	409.0	396.7	368.0	291.0

Harry Potter and the Deathly Hallows: Part 2

On July 15, 2011, fans rushed to theaters to see *Harry Potter and the Deathly Hallows: Part 2*, spending $91 million in a single day. It was released in 4,375 theaters and earned an average of $20,816 per location. The final film in the wizard franchise went on to earn $1.3 billion worldwide—making it the fourth-highest-grossing movie of all time. It also holds the film record for earning $150 million in the shortest amount of time. *Harry Potter and the Deathly Hallows: Part 2* was nominated for three Academy Awards in 2011—Art Direction, Visual Effects, and Makeup.

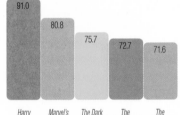

movies that earned the most in a single day

box-office earnings,
in millions of US dollars

91.0	80.8	75.7	72.7	71.6
Harry Potter and the Deathly Hallows: Part 2, 7/15/11	Marvel's The Avengers, 5/4/12	The Dark Knight Rises, 7/20/12	The Twilight Saga: New Moon, 11/20/09	The Twilight Saga: Breaking Dawn—Part 1, 11/18/11

top-selling dvd of 2013

The Twilight Saga: Breaking Dawn, Part 1

More than 4.8 million fans flocked to stores in 2013 to purchase a DVD copy of *The Twilight Saga: Breaking Dawn, Part 1*. The first part of the hugely successful franchise's finale hit theaters in November 2011 and claimed the fifth-highest opening day total in history with $71.6 million. During its run, it brought in $709 million worldwide. In the film, Bella (Kristen Stewart) and Edward (Robert Pattinson) are married and begin their new life together—against the wishes of Bella's friend Jacob Black (Taylor Lautner).

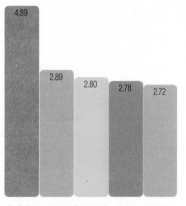

top-selling dvds of 2013

units sold, in millions

4.89	2.89	2.80	2.78	2.72
The Twilight Saga: Breaking Dawn, Part 1	Wreck-It Ralph	The Hobbit: An Unexpected Journey	Hotel Transylvania	Pitch Perfect

bestselling movie soundtrack
The Bodyguard

The soundtrack of *The Bodyguard* has sold more than 17 million copies since it was released in November 1992. The movie starred Kevin Costner as a former secret service agent in charge of a pop singer, played by Whitney Houston. Houston produced the soundtrack, along with Clive Davis, and it features three of Houston's biggest hits—"I Will Always Love You," "I Have Nothing," and "I'm Every Woman." The album picked up a Grammy for Album of the Year and reached number one on music charts worldwide, including Australia, Canada, France, Germany, and Japan.

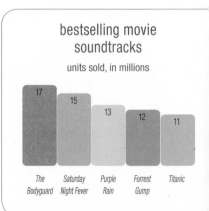

bestselling movie soundtracks
units sold, in millions

The Bodyguard	Saturday Night Fever	Purple Rain	Forrest Gump	Titanic
17	15	13	12	11

united states' bestselling recording group

The Beatles

The Beatles have sold 177 million copies of their albums in the United States since their first official recording session in September 1962. In the two years that followed, they had 26 Top 40 singles. John Lennon, Paul McCartney, George Harrison, and Ringo Starr made up the "Fab Four," as the Beatles were known. Together they recorded many albums that are now considered rock masterpieces, such as *Rubber Soul, Sgt. Pepper's Lonely Hearts Club Band,* and *The Beatles.* The group broke up in 1969. In 2001, however, their newly released greatest hits album—*The Beatles 1*—reached the top of the charts. One of their best-known songs—"Yesterday"—is the most-recorded song in history, with about 2,500 different artists recording their own versions.

united states' bestselling recording groups

albums sold, in millions

The Beatles	Led Zeppelin	The Eagles	Pink Floyd	AC/DC
177.0	111.5	100.0	74.5	71.5

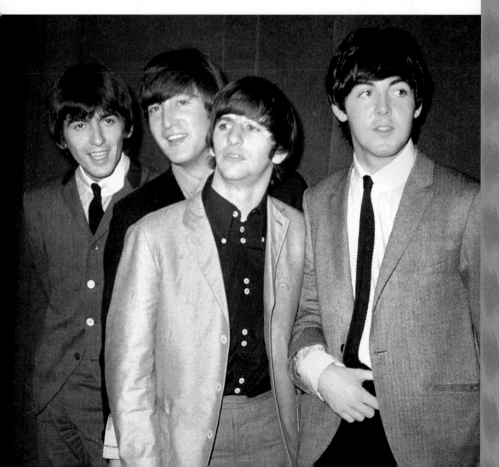

top-selling recording artist of 2013

Justin Timberlake

Justine Timberlake sold more than 3.4 million albums in 2013. During the year, he released two albums—*The 20/20 Experience* (March) and *The 20/20 Experience—2 of 2* (September). Both debuted at number one on the Billboard 200 chart. To promote the albums, Timberlake took part in *Legends of the Summer Stadium Tour with Jay-Z*, as well as *The 20/20 Experience World Tour*. Some of Timberlake's past albums, which are included in the total annual sales, include *Justified* (2002) and *FutureSex/LoveSounds* (2006).

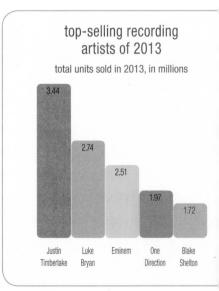

top-selling recording artists of 2013

total units sold in 2013, in millions

Justin Timberlake	Luke Bryan	Eminem	One Direction	Blake Shelton
3.44	2.74	2.51	1.97	1.72

most downloaded song
"Blurred Lines"

"Blurred Lines" by Robin Thicke (featuring Pharrell Williams and TI) was downloaded almost 6.5 million times in 2013. That's enough for everyone in the entire state of Tennessee to have a copy. It sold more than 5 million copies in just 22 weeks—faster than any other digital song in history. Although the song hit the charts at number 94, it quickly jumped in popularity after Thicke and Williams performed it on NBC's *The Voice*. It became Thicke's first song to top the Billboard Hot 100 chart and also peaked at number 1 in 14 other countries, including Ireland, Spain, Germany, Australia, Canada, and the UK. The video was released in March 2013.

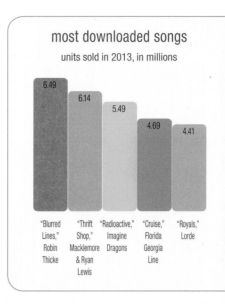

most downloaded songs
units sold in 2013, in millions

"Blurred Lines," Robin Thicke	6.49
"Thrift Shop," Macklemore & Ryan Lewis	6.14
"Radioactive," Imagine Dragons	5.49
"Cruise," Florida Georgia Line	4.69
"Royals," Lorde	4.41

most-streamed song

Harlem Shake

The catchy dance song "Harlem Shake" by American DJ Baauer was streamed more than 489 million times in 2013. That's 1.33 million times a day, or 15.5 times each second! Although the song was first released in May 2012, it did not become popular until February 2013 when it was featured in a YouTube video. After that, it was the top-rated song on the Billboard Hot 100 for five straight weeks. It also reached number one in Australia, Greece, New Zealand, Luxembourg, and the UK.

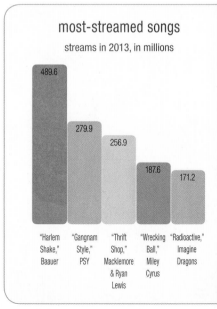

most-streamed songs
streams in 2013, in millions

Song	Streams
"Harlem Shake," Baauer	489.6
"Gangnam Style," PSY	279.9
"Thrift Shop," Macklemore & Ryan Lewis	256.9
"Wrecking Ball," Miley Cyrus	187.6
"Radioactive," Imagine Dragons	171.2

top selling digital album of all time

21

Adele's *21* is the bestselling digital album of all time with 3 million downloads. The album debuted at number one on the Billboard 200, and stayed in the top five for 39 consecutive weeks. Some of the album's most-successful songs include "Rolling in the Deep," "Someone Like You," "Set Fire to the Rain," and "Rumour Has It." In 2012, Adele won seven Grammy Awards for *21*, including Album of the Year and Best Pop Vocal Album. It also won the BRIT Award for British Album of the Year. This was the singer's second studio album, and it was released in January 2011.

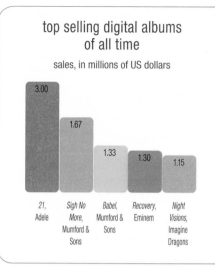

top selling digital albums of all time

sales, in millions of US dollars

21, Adele	Sigh No More, Mumford & Sons	Babel, Mumford & Sons	Recovery, Eminem	Night Visions, Imagine Dragons
3.00	1.67	1.33	1.30	1.15

bestselling digital song of all time

"I Gotta Feeling"

The Black Eyed Peas' mega dance hit "I Gotta Feeling" is the bestselling digital song of all time, with more than 8.4 million downloads. The song, which was released in May 2009, is from The Black Eyed Peas' fifth studio album, *The E.N.D.* "I Gotta Feeling" won a Grammy Award for Best Pop Performance by a Duo or Group, and was nominated for Song of the Year at the World Music Awards. The song was number one on the Billboard Hot 100 chart for 12 straight weeks and also topped music charts in 25 other countries. The members of the group are will.i.am, apl.de.ap, Taboo, and Fergie.

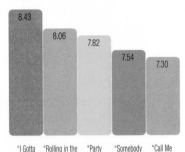

bestselling digital songs of all time

units sold, in millions

"I Gotta Feeling," The Black Eyed Peas	"Rolling in the Deep," Adele	"Party Rock Anthem," LMFAO	"Somebody That I Used to Know," Gotye	"Call Me Maybe," Carly Rae Jepsen
8.43	8.06	7.82	7.54	7.30

top-earning deceased musician
Michael Jackson

Even though Michael Jackson passed away in June 2009, he's still earning a ton of cash. In fact, in the 12 months following his death, he sold 35 million albums worldwide. In 2013, Jackson's sales and royalties from past projects brought in $160 million—almost twice as much as the next three earners combined. In 2013, Cirque du Soleil created a show called *Michael Jackson: One* in Las Vegas. During his impressive career, Jackson made 10 solo albums, including *Thriller*—the bestselling album of all time. He also won 13 Grammy Awards and 26 American Music Awards.

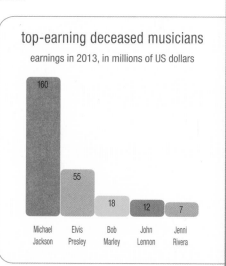

top-earning deceased musicians
earnings in 2013, in millions of US dollars

Michael Jackson	Elvis Presley	Bob Marley	John Lennon	Jenni Rivera
160	55	18	12	7

bestselling digital album

20/20 Experience

Justin Timberlake's *The 20/20 Experience* was the bestselling digital album of 2013 with more than 1 million downloads. The album's extremely successful singles include "Suit & Tie" (featuring Jay-Z) and "Mirrors." Timberlake performed "Suit & Tie" at the 2013 Grammy Awards, and at a televised concert the night before the Super Bowl. *The 20/20 Experience* was Timberlake's third studio album, and was followed by *The 20/20 Experience—2 of 2*. Together, the two albums were nominated for a Grammy Award for Best Pop Vocal Album.

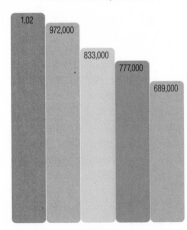

bestselling digital albums
units sold in 2013, in millions

Album	Units
The 20/20 Experience, Justin Timberlake	1.02
Beyoncé, Beyoncé	972,000
Night Visions, Imagine Dragons	833,000
Marshall Mathers LP2, Eminem	777,000
Nothing Was the Same, Drake	689,000

most-watched music video
"Gentlemen"

YouTube ranked the most-watched music videos of 2013, and PSY's "Gentlemen" came in at number one. The South Korean singer, who achieved international fame with his hit "Gangnam Style," entertained viewers again with his signature dance moves. More than 18.9 million people viewed it when the video debuted on April 13, 2013, setting a YouTube record. Three days later, it had been seen by more than 70 million people. PSY performed the song on the finales of *Dancing with the Stars* and *Britain's Got Talent*. The song is also included on the Just Dance 2014 video game.

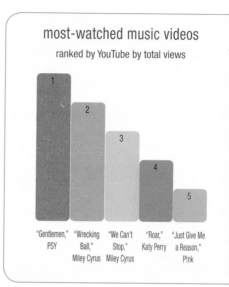

most-watched music videos
ranked by YouTube by total views

1 — "Gentlemen," PSY
2 — "Wrecking Ball," Miley Cyrus
3 — "We Can't Stop," Miley Cyrus
4 — "Roar," Katy Perry
5 — "Just Give Me a Reason," P!nk

top-earning male singer

Toby Keith

Country singer-songwriter Toby Keith earned $65 million during 2013. Keith released his sixteenth studio album—*Hope on the Rocks*—in October 2012, and it produced two top-20 hits. In June 2013, Keith released another studio album, titled *Drinks After Work,* which produced a single by the same name. He also embarked on the *Hammer Down Tour* to promote his album. In addition to being a successful musician, Keith is also involved in several profitable businesses, including a few restaurants and a clothing line called TK Steelman.

top-earning male singers
income in 2013, in millions of US dollars

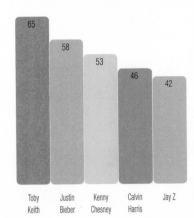

Toby Keith	Justin Bieber	Kenny Chesney	Calvin Harris	Jay Z
65	58	53	46	42

top-earning female singer

Madonna

During 2013, music legend Madonna pulled in $125 million! Most of the singer's cash came from her 2012 album *MDNA*, and her world tour by the same name. It was Madonna's twelfth studio album, and it debuted at number one in the United States, the UK, Canada, and several other countries. The album's first single, "Give Me All Your Luvin'," became Madonna's 38th top-ten hit— the most in Billboard 100's history. The MDNA Tour, which lasted from May to December 2012, earned about $305 million, and was one of the top-15 highest-grossing tours of all time.

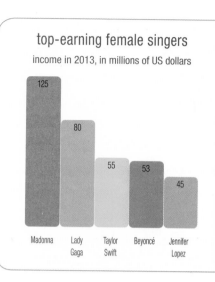

top-earning female singers
income in 2013, in millions of US dollars

Madonna	Lady Gaga	Taylor Swift	Beyoncé	Jennifer Lopez
125	80	55	53	45

most-played song
"Blurred Lines"

The catchy dance song "Blurred Lines" by Robin Thicke was played on the radio more than 672,660 times during 2013. That breaks down to about 76.5 times an hour. The song also featured rapper TI and singer/producer Pharrell Williams. It was the lead single off Thicke's *Blurred Lines* album and was released in March 2013. It reached number one on the Billboard Hot 100 and stayed there for 12 consecutive weeks. "Blurred Lines" was nominated for two Grammy Awards— Record of the Year and Best Pop Duo/ Group Performance.

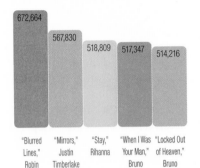

most-played songs
radio detections in 2013

"Blurred Lines," Robin Thicke	"Mirrors," Justin Timberlake	"Stay," Rihanna	"When I Was Your Man," Bruno Mars	"Locked Out of Heaven," Bruno Mars
672,664	567,830	518,809	517,347	514,216

musician with the most mtv video music awards

Madonna

Madonna has won 20 MTV Video Music Awards since the ceremony was first held in 1984. She has won four Cinematography awards, three Female Video awards, three Directing awards, two Editing awards, and two Art Direction awards. She also picked up single awards for Video of the Year, Choreography, Special Effects, and Long Form Video, as well as a Viewer's Choice and a Video Vanguard Award. Madonna's award-winning videos include "Papa Don't Preach," "Like a Prayer," "Express Yourself," "Vogue," "Rain," "Take a Bow," "Ray of Light," and "Beautiful Stranger."

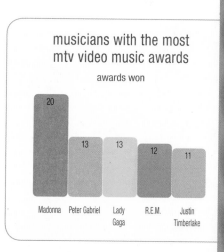

musicians with the most mtv video music awards

awards won

Madonna	Peter Gabriel	Lady Gaga	R.E.M.	Justin Timberlake
20	13	13	12	11

113

top-earning tour

Bon Jovi

Veteran rockers Bon Jovi had the top tour of 2013, hauling in more than $295 million dollars. The group's *Because We Can: The Tour* kicked off in February 2013 and ran through December with 102 shows worldwide—61 in North America and 42 international stops. The tour promoted the group's twelfth studio album, *What About Now*. The set list included new material such as "That's What the Water Made Me" and "Because We Can," but also featured some Bon Jovi classics like "You Give Love a Bad Name," "Bad Medicine," and "Born to Be My Baby."

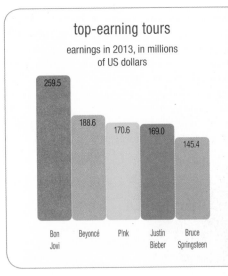

top-earning tours

earnings in 2013, in millions of US dollars

Bon Jovi	Beyoncé	P!nk	Justin Bieber	Bruce Springsteen
259.5	188.6	170.6	169.0	145.4

act with the most country music awards

George Strait

George Strait has won a whopping 23 Country Music Awards and has been nicknamed the "King of Country" for all of his accomplishments in the business. He won his first CMA in 1985, and his most recent in 2013. In addition to his many awards, Strait holds the record for the most number one hits on the Billboard Hot Country Songs with 44. He also has 38 hit albums, including 13 multiplatinum and 33 platinum records. He was inducted into the Country Music Hall of Fame in 2006.

acts with the most
country music awards

awards won

George Strait	Brooks & Dunn	Vince Gill	Alan Jackson	Miranda Lambert
23	19	18	16	16

115

longest-running broadway show

The Phantom of the Opera

The Phantom of the Opera has been performed more than 10,847 times since it opened in January 1988. The show tells the story of a disfigured musical genius who terrorizes the performers of the Paris Opera House. More than 130 million people have seen a performance in 145 cities and 27 countries. The show won seven Tony Awards during its opening year, including Best Musical. The musical drama is performed at the Majestic Theater.

longest-running broadway shows
total performances*

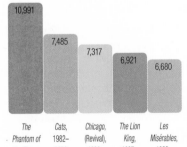

10,991	7,485	7,317	6,921	6,680
The Phantom of the Opera, 1988–	Cats, 1982–2000	Chicago, (Revival), 1996–	The Lion King, 1997–	Les Misérables, 1982–2000

*As of July 2014

musical with the most tony awards

The Producers

In March 2001, *The Producers* took home 12 of its record-breaking 15 Tony Award nominations. The Broadway smash won awards for Musical, Original Score, Book, Direction of a Musical, Choreography, Orchestration, Scenic Design, Costume Design, Lighting Design, Actor in a Musical, Featured Actor in a Musical, and Actress in a Musical. *The Producers*, which originally starred Nathan Lane and Matthew Broderick, is a stage adaptation of Mel Brooks's 1968 movie. Brooks wrote the lyrics and music for 16 new songs for the stage version.

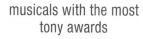

musicals with the most tony awards
awards won

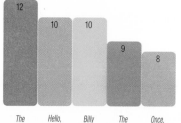

The Producers, 2001	Hello, Dolly! 1964	Billy Elliot, 2009	The Book of Mormon, 2011	Once, 2007
12	10	10	9	8

Nature Records

natural formations
animals
weather
plants
disasters
environment

Any Which Way But Up

Flamingos can only eat with their heads upside down. When the bird sticks its head in the water, there are two holes in the top beak that act as a strainer. The flamingo's tongue then pushes water in and out of its mouth three or four times a second, hoping to catch brine shrimp, insects, and fish.

The Nose Knows

Dog nose prints are as individual as human fingerprints, and can be used to identify lost or stolen canines. Dog noses also have an unusual method of picking up scents. The nose has a thin layer of mucus that allows chemicals in the air to dissolve there and absorb into the skin where scent-detecting cells are located.

Flower Power

The bladderwort plant lives most of its life underwater. But when it's time to flower, the plant inflates its air sacs and rises to the surface. The bladderwort stands about 8 inches (20 cm) tall, and only lives for a season. The plant is also unique because the leaves below the plant can trap and digest small fish for food.

That Rocks

Some of the fastest meteorites can travel through space at about 26 miles (42 km) per second. About 500 meteorites make it to Earth each year, but only about 5 of those will be studied by scientists. It's estimated that about 48.5 tons (44 tn) of meteoritic debris hit Earth each day. The largest meteor to hit Earth touched down in southwest Africa and weighed 119,000 pounds (54,000 kg).

Light Bright

Rainbows are made up of millions of water droplets through which light is reflected, and there are a few unusual variations. Double rainbows occur when light reflects twice within the water droplet, causing a second, fainter rainbow beneath the main one. Occasionally, the light will reflect three or four times, creating multiple rainbows. On very rare occasions, moonbows—or lunar rainbows—occur by the light of the moon, but are very faint.

Watermelon Snow

In parts of the Sierra Nevada Mountains in California, and parts of the alpine region of Colorado, it's possible to see pink snow. This phenomenon occurs when microscopic algae that dwell in cold climates mix with the precipitation. It is also sometimes called "watermelon snow" because the algae give off a sweet scent.

Fabulous Fossil Find

One of the largest dinosaur graveyards ever discovered exists in the Patagonia region of southern Chile and contains almost 50 entire ichthyosaur skeletons. These dinos were dolphin-like creatures that lived between 90 to 245 million years ago. The fossils found range from newborn to one reaching 16 feet (4.8 m) long. The site, which was discovered in May 2014, is only reachable by a 14-hour hike.

largest diamond
Golden Jubilee

The Golden Jubilee is the world's largest faceted diamond, with a weight of 545.67 carats. This gigantic gem got its name when it was presented to the king of Thailand in 1997 for the Golden Jubilee—or 50th anniversary celebration—of his reign. The diamond weighed 755.5 carats when it was discovered in a South African mine in 1986. Once it was cut, the diamond featured 148 perfectly symmetrical facets. The process took almost a year because of the diamond's size and multiple tension points. The diamond is on display at the Royal Museum of Bangkok in Thailand.

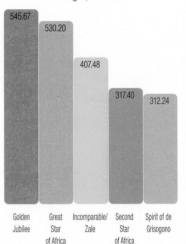

largest diamonds
weight, in carats

Golden Jubilee	Great Star of Africa	Incomparable/ Zale	Second Star of Africa	Spirit of de Grisogono
545.67	530.20	407.48	317.40	312.24

tallest mountain

Mount Everest

Mount Everest's tallest peak towers 29,035 feet (8,850 m) into the air, and it is the highest point on Earth. This peak is an unbelievable 5.5 miles (8.8 km) above sea level. Mount Everest is located in the Himalayas, on the border between Nepal and Tibet. The mountain got its official name from surveyor Sir George Everest. In 1953, Sir Edmund Hillary and Tenzing Norgay were the first people to reach the peak. In 2008, the Olympic torch was carried up to the top of the mountain on its way to the games in Beijing.

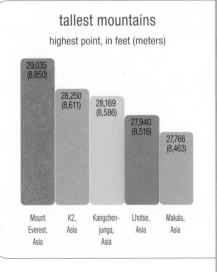

tallest mountains
highest point, in feet (meters)

Mount Everest, Asia	K2, Asia	Kangchen-junga, Asia	Lhotse, Asia	Makalu, Asia
29,035 (8,850)	28,250 (8,611)	28,169 (8,586)	27,940 (8,516)	27,766 (8,463)

largest lake

Caspian Sea

This giant inland body of salt water stretches for almost 750 miles (1,207 km) from north to south, with an average width of about 200 miles (322 km). Altogether, it covers 143,200 square miles (370,901 sq km). The Caspian Sea is located east of the Caucasus Mountains in central Asia. It is bordered by Iran, Russia, Kazakhstan, Azerbaijan, and Turkmenistan. The Caspian Sea has an average depth of about 550 feet (170 m). It is an important fishing resource, with species including sturgeon, salmon, perch, herring, and carp. Other animals living in the Caspian Sea include porpoises, seals, and tortoises. The sea is estimated to be 30 million years old and became landlocked 5.5 million years ago.

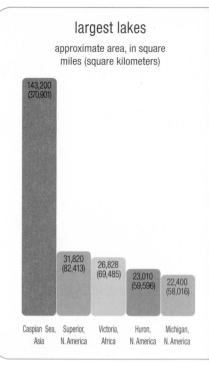

largest lakes

approximate area, in square miles (square kilometers)

Caspian Sea, Asia	Superior, N. America	Victoria, Africa	Huron, N. America	Michigan, N. America
143,200 (370,901)	31,820 (82,413)	26,828 (69,485)	23,010 (59,596)	22,400 (58,016)

largest desert

Sahara

Located in northern Africa, the Sahara desert covers approximately 3.5 million square miles (9.1 million sq km). It stretches for 5,200 miles (8,372 km) through the countries of Morocco, Algeria, Tunisia, Libya, Egypt, Mauritania, Mali, Niger, Chad, and Sudan. The Sahara gets very little rainfall—less than 8 inches (20 cm) per year. Even with its harsh environment, some 2.5 million people—mostly nomads—call the Sahara home. Date palms and acacias grow near oases. Some of the animals that live in the Sahara include gazelles, antelopes, jackals, foxes, and badgers.

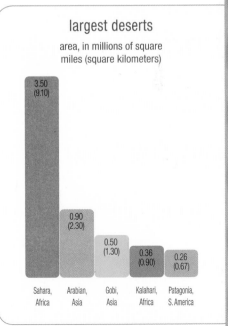

largest deserts

area, in millions of square miles (square kilometers)

Desert	Area
Sahara, Africa	3.50 (9.10)
Arabian, Asia	0.90 (2.30)
Gobi, Asia	0.50 (1.30)
Kalahari, Africa	0.36 (0.90)
Patagonia, S. America	0.26 (0.67)

125

longest river

Nile

The Nile River in Africa stretches 4,145 miles (6,671 km) from the tributaries of Lake Victoria in Tanzania and Uganda out to the Mediterranean Sea. Because of varying depths, ships can sail on only about 2,000 miles (3,217 km) of the river. The Nile flows through Rwanda, Uganda, Sudan, and Egypt. The river's water supply is crucial to the existence of these African countries. The Nile's precious water is used to irrigate crops and to generate electricity. The Aswan Dam and the Aswan High Dam—both located in Egypt—are used to store the autumn floodwater for later use. The Nile is also used to transport goods from city to city along the river.

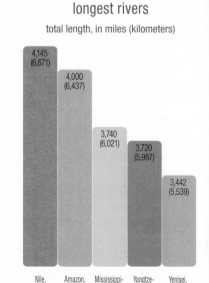

longest rivers
total length, in miles (kilometers)

River	Length
Nile, Africa	4,145 (6,671)
Amazon, S. America	4,000 (6,437)
Mississippi-Missouri, N. America	3,740 (6,021)
Yangtze-Kiang, Asia	3,720 (5,987)
Yenisei, Asia	3,442 (5,539)

largest ocean
Pacific

The Pacific Ocean covers almost 64 million square miles (166 million sq km) and reaches 36,200 feet (11,000 m) below sea level at its greatest depth—the Mariana Trench (near the Philippines). In fact, this ocean is so large that it covers about one-third of the planet (more than all of Earth's land put together) and holds more than half of all the seawater on Earth. The United States could fit inside this ocean 18 times! Some of the major bodies of water included in the Pacific are the Bering Sea, the Coral Sea, the Philippine Sea, and the Gulf of Alaska.

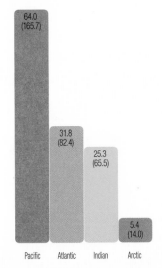

largest oceans

approximate area, in millions of square miles (square kilometers)

Pacific	Atlantic	Indian	Arctic
64.0 (165.7)	31.8 (82.4)	25.3 (65.5)	5.4 (14.0)

largest coral reef

Great Barrier Reef

The Great Barrier Reef stretches for some 1,429 miles (2,300 km) in the Coral Sea along the coast of Australia. It's larger than the Great Wall of China, and it's the only living thing that can be seen from space. More than 3,000 individual reef systems and coral cays make up this intricate structure. A large part of the reef makes up Great Barrier Reef Marine Park, which helps to preserve the area by limiting fishing, tourism, and human use. Thousands of animal species are supported by the reef, including 600 species of fish, 450 species of hard coral, and about 30 species of dolphins and whales. The Great Barrier Reef is considered a World Heritage Site, and one of the Seven Natural Wonders of the World.

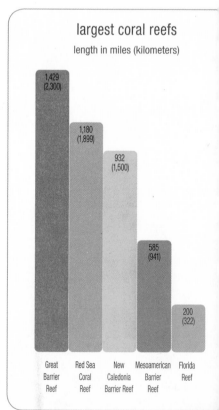

largest coral reefs
length in miles (kilometers)

Great Barrier Reef	Red Sea Coral Reef	New Caledonia Barrier Reef	Mesoamerican Barrier Reef	Florida Reef
1,429 (2,300)	1,180 (1,899)	932 (1,500)	585 (941)	200 (322)

deepest sea trench

Mariana Trench

Located in the Pacific Ocean near Japan, the Mariana Trench is the deepest opening in Earth's crust at 35,787 feet (10,907 m)—that's almost 7 miles (11.2 km). Mount Everest—the world's tallest mountain at 29,035 feet (8,850 m)—could easily fit inside. The deepest point in the trench is called the Challenger Deep, named after oceanographer Jacques Piccard's exploration vessel, which first mapped the location in 1951. The trench is home to many types of crabs and fish, as well as more than 200 different types of microorganisms.

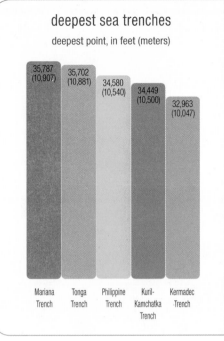

deepest sea trenches

deepest point, in feet (meters)

Mariana Trench	Tonga Trench	Philippine Trench	Kuril-Kamchatka Trench	Kermadec Trench
35,787 (10,907)	35,702 (10,881)	34,580 (10,540)	34,449 (10,500)	32,963 (10,047)

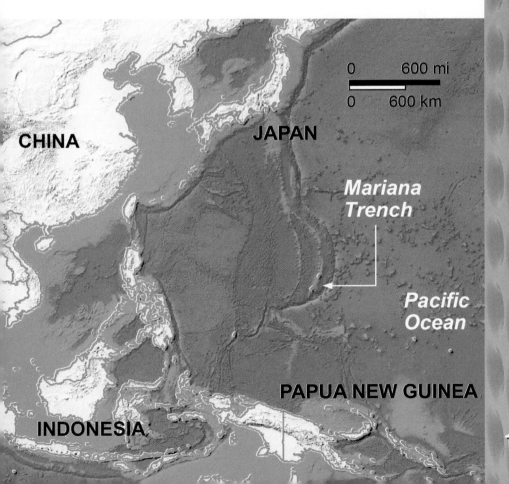

CHINA

JAPAN

Mariana Trench

Pacific Ocean

PAPUA NEW GUINEA

INDONESIA

0 — 600 mi
0 — 600 km

largest crustacean

Giant Spider Crab

The giant spider crab has up to a 12-foot (3.7 m) leg span. That's almost wide enough to take up two parking spaces! The crab's body measures about 15 inches (38.1 cm) wide. Its ten long legs are jointed, and the first pair has large claws at the end. The giant sea creature can weigh 35–44 pounds (16–20 kg). It feeds on dead animals and shellfish it finds on the ocean floor. Giant spider crabs live in the deep water of the Pacific Ocean off southern Japan.

largest crustaceans
leg span, in feet (meters)

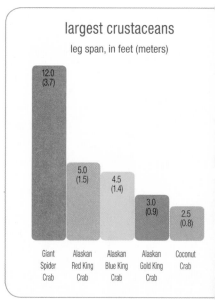

Giant Spider Crab	Alaskan Red King Crab	Alaskan Blue King Crab	Alaskan Gold King Crab	Coconut Crab
12.0 (3.7)	5.0 (1.5)	4.5 (1.4)	3.0 (0.9)	2.5 (0.8)

largest cephalopod

Colossal Squid

Living up to 6,000 feet (1,829 m) deep in the Antarctic Ocean, the colossal squid can grow to a length of 46 feet (14 m). That's about the same size as three SUVs! The squid, which is very rarely seen by people, can weigh about 1,500 pounds (681 kg). Its eyes are the size of dinner plates, and are the largest eyes in the animal kingdom. The colossal squid uses its 20-foot (6 m) long tentacles to catch its prey. In addition to the two tentacles, this giant cephalopod has eight arms. In the center of its body, the squid has a razor-sharp beak that it uses to shred its prey before eating it.

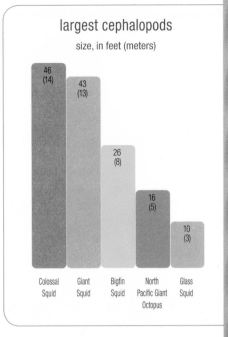

largest cephalopods
size, in feet (meters)

Colossal Squid	Giant Squid	Bigfin Squid	North Pacific Giant Octopus	Glass Squid
46 (14)	43 (13)	26 (8)	16 (5)	10 (3)

most dangerous shark

Great White

With a total of 249 known unprovoked attacks on humans, great white sharks are the most dangerous predators in the sea. A great white can measure more than 20 feet (6.1 m) in length and weigh 5,000 pounds (2,268 kg) or more. Because of the sharks' size, they can feed on large prey, including seals, dolphins, and even small whales. Often, when a human is attacked by a great white, it is because the shark has mistaken the person for its typical prey. The sharks make their homes in most waters throughout the world, but are most frequently found off the coasts of Australia, South Africa, California, and Mexico.

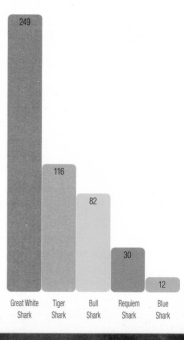

most dangerous sharks
number of unprovoked attacks

Great White Shark	Tiger Shark	Bull Shark	Requiem Shark	Blue Shark
249	116	82	30	12

biggest fish
Whale Shark

Although the average length of a whale shark is 30 feet (9 m), many have been known to reach up to 60 feet (18 m) long. That's the same length as two school buses! Whale sharks also weigh an average of 50,000 pounds (22,680 kg). As with most sharks, the females are larger than the males. Their mouths measure about 5 feet (1.5 m) long and contain about 3,000 teeth. Amazingly, these gigantic fish eat only microscopic plankton and tiny fish. They float near the surface looking for food.

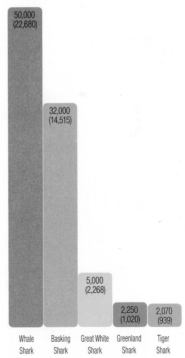

biggest fish
average weight, in pounds (kilograms)

Whale Shark	Basking Shark	Great White Shark	Greenland Shark	Tiger Shark
50,000 (22,680)	32,000 (14,515)	5,000 (2,268)	2,250 (1,020)	2,070 (939)

fastest fish
Sailfish

A sailfish once grabbed a fishing line and dragged it 300 feet (91 m) away in just three seconds. That means it was swimming at an average speed of 69 miles (109 km) per hour—higher than the average speed limit on a highway! Sailfish are very large—they average 6 feet (1.8 m) long, but can grow up to 11 feet (3.4 m). They eat squid and surface-dwelling fish, and sometimes several sailfish will work together to catch their prey. They are found in both the Atlantic and Pacific oceans and prefer a water temperature of about 80°F (27°C).

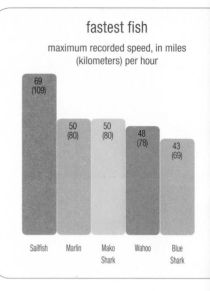

fastest fish
maximum recorded speed, in miles (kilometers) per hour

Sailfish	Marlin	Mako Shark	Wahoo	Blue Shark
69 (109)	50 (80)	50 (80)	48 (78)	43 (69)

biggest dolphin

Orca

Although they are known as *killer whales*, the orca is actually a member of the dolphin family and can measure up to 32 feet (9.7 m) in length and weigh up to 6 tons (5.4 t). These powerful marine mammals are carnivores with 4-inch (1.6 cm) long teeth, and they feed mainly on seals, sea lions, and smaller whales. Orcas live in pods of up to 40 other whales, and pod members help one another round up prey. Killer whales can live for up to 80 years and are highly intelligent.

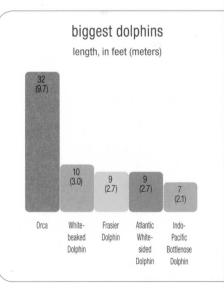

biggest dolphins
length, in feet (meters)

Orca	White-beaked Dolphin	Frasier Dolphin	Atlantic White-sided Dolphin	Indo-Pacific Bottlenose Dolphin
32 (9.7)	10 (3.0)	9 (2.7)	9 (2.7)	7 (2.1)

135

heaviest marine mammal

Blue Whale

Blue whales are the largest animals that have ever inhabited Earth. They can weigh more than 143.3 tons (130 t) and measure over 100 feet (30 m) long. Amazingly, these gentle giants only eat krill—small shrimplike animals. A blue whale can eat about 4 tons (3.6 t) of krill each day in the summer, when food is plentiful. To catch the krill, a whale gulps as much as 17,000 gallons (64,600 L) of seawater into its mouth at one time. Then it uses its tongue—which can be as big as a car—to push the water back out. The krill get caught in hairs on the whale's baleen (a keratin filtering structure that hangs down from the roof of the whale's mouth).

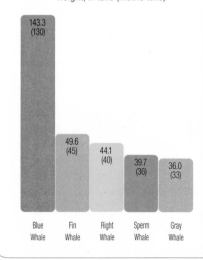

heaviest marine mammals
weight, in tons (metric tons)

Blue Whale	Fin Whale	Right Whale	Sperm Whale	Gray Whale
143.3 (130)	49.6 (45)	44.1 (40)	39.7 (36)	36.0 (33)

marine mammal with the largest brain

Sperm Whale

The sperm whale's brain is the largest marine mammal brain in the world, weighing more than 17 pounds (7.7 kg). That's more than five times the size of a human brain. Sperm whales can grow to about 60 feet (18 m) long and weigh up to 45 tons (41 t). The head makes up about one-third of the animal's body. Sperm whales can also dive deeper than any other whale, reaching depths of 3,300 feet (1,006 m) in search of squid. They can eat about 1 ton (0.9 t) of fish and squid daily. Sperm whales can be found in all oceans, and they generally live in pods of about a dozen adults and their offspring.

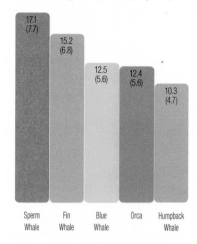

marine mammals with the largest brains

brain weight, in pounds (kilograms)

Sperm Whale	Fin Whale	Blue Whale	Orca	Humpback Whale
17.1 (7.7)	15.2 (6.8)	12.5 (5.6)	12.4 (5.6)	10.3 (4.7)

largest bird wingspan

Marabou Stork

With a wingspan that can reach up to 13 feet (4 m), the marabou stork has the largest wingspan of any bird. These large storks weigh up to 20 pounds (9 kg) and can grow up to 5 feet (150 cm) tall. Their long leg bones and toe bones are actually hollow. This adaptation is very important for flight because it makes the bird lighter. Although marabous eat insects, small mammals, and fish, the majority of their food is carrion—meat that is already dead. In fact, the stork's head and neck do not have any feathers. This helps the bird stay clean as it sticks its head into carcasses to pick out scraps of food.

largest bird wingspans
wingspan, in feet (meters)

Marabou Stork	Albatross	Trumpeter Swan	Mute Swan	Whooper Swan
13 (4.0)	12 (3.7)	11 (3.4)	10 (3.0)	10 (3.0)

biggest penguin

Emperor Penguin

Emperor penguins are giants among their species, growing to a height of 44 inches (111.7 cm) and weighing up to 80 pounds (37 kg). These penguins are the only animals that spend the entire winter on the open ice in Antarctica, withstanding temperatures as low as -75°F (-60°C). The female penguin lays a 1-pound (0.5 kg) egg on the ice, and then goes off to hunt for weeks at a time. The male penguin scoops up the egg, and keeps it warm on his feet below his toasty belly. When the eggs hatch, the females return with food.

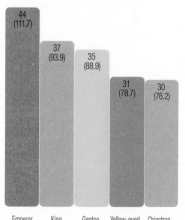

biggest penguins
height in inches (centimeters)

Emperor Penguin	King Penguin	Gentoo Penguin	Yellow-eyed Penguin	Chinstrap Penguin
44 (111.7)	37 (93.9)	35 (88.9)	31 (78.7)	30 (76.2)

largest owl

Blakiston's Fish Owl

A female Blakiston's fish owl can measure up to 3 feet (.9 m) high, weigh up to 10 pounds (4.5 kg), and have a 6-foot (1.8 m) wingspan. Females are larger than males. As its name suggests, the Blakiston's fish owl primarily eats fish—including pike, trout, and salmon—and can catch a meal that weighs almost as much as the owl itself. These birds live and nest in old-growth forests along coastlines throughout Japan and Russia. However, due to forest clearing and other threats to its habitat, the Blakiston's fish owl is endangered.

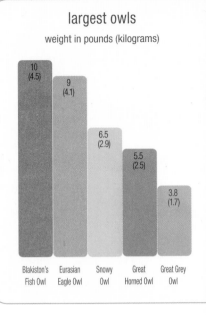

largest owls

weight in pounds (kilograms)

Blakiston's Fish Owl	Eurasian Eagle Owl	Snowy Owl	Great Horned Owl	Great Grey Owl
10 (4.5)	9 (4.1)	6.5 (2.9)	5.5 (2.5)	3.8 (1.7)

A pair of juvenile bald eagles near their nest

bird that builds the largest nest

Bald Eagle

With a nest that can measure 8 feet (2.4 m) wide and 16 feet (4.9 m) deep, bald eagles have plenty of room to move around. These birds of prey have wingspans of up to 7.5 feet (2.3 m) and need a home that they can nest in comfortably. By carefully constructing their nest with sticks, branches, and plant material, a pair of bald eagles can balance their home—which can weigh up to 4,000 pounds (1,814 kg)—on the top of a tree or cliff. These nests are usually located by rivers or coastlines, the birds' watery hunting grounds. Called an aerie, this home will be used for the rest of the eagles' lives.

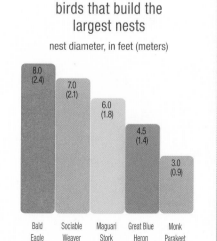

birds that build the largest nests

nest diameter, in feet (meters)

8.0 (2.4)	7.0 (2.1)	6.0 (1.8)	4.5 (1.4)	3.0 (0.9)
Bald Eagle	Sociable Weaver	Maguari Stork	Great Blue Heron	Monk Parakeet

largest bird egg

Ostrich Egg

Ostriches—the world's largest birds—can lay eggs that measure 5 inches by 6 inches (13 cm by 16 cm) and weigh up to 4 pounds (1.8 kg). In fact, just one ostrich egg weighs as much as 24 chicken eggs! The egg yolk makes up one-third of the volume. Although the eggshell is only 0.08 inches (2 mm) thick, it is tough enough to withstand the weight of a 345-pound (157 kg) ostrich. An ostrich hen can lay from 10 to 70 eggs each year. Females are usually able to recognize their own eggs, even when they are mixed in with those of other females in their shared nest.

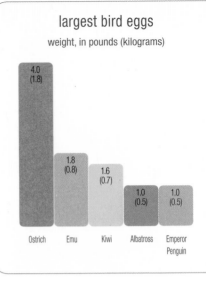

largest bird eggs

weight, in pounds (kilograms)

4.0 (1.8)	1.8 (0.8)	1.6 (0.7)	1.0 (0.5)	1.0 (0.5)
Ostrich	Emu	Kiwi	Albatross	Emperor Penguin

Sockeye salmon

most endangered
US animal group

Fish

There are 83 species of fish that are currently endangered in the United States. A species is considered endangered if it is in danger of becoming extinct. In addition, there are another 71 fish species that are considered threatened. Out of the 154 endangered and threatened fish species, there is a recovery plan in place for 103 of them. The main reasons for the decline in some species' populations are overfishing, water pollution, and loss of habitat. Some of the most well-known endangered fish include the Atlantic salmon, the steelhead trout, the sockeye salmon, and the Atlantic sturgeon.

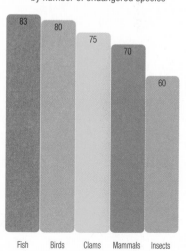

most endangered US animal groups

by number of endangered species

Fish	Birds	Clams	Mammals	Insects
83	80	75	70	60

sleepiest animal

Koala

Awake for just 2 hours a day, the koala is the sleepiest animal on earth. This means that the marsupial is asleep for about 8,000 hours a year! Koalas are found in eastern Australia, and spend most of the day snoozing and feeding in eucalyptus trees. They eat about 2.5 pounds (1.1 kg) of leaves a day. Koalas rarely need to drink because they get most of their water from the trees' juicy leaves. Although eucalyptus leaves cannot be eaten by humans, koalas have a special digestive system that allows them to easily digest the toxic oil in the foliage. In the wild, these mammals can live for up to 20 years.

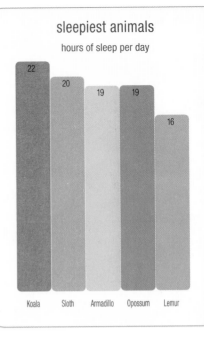

sleepiest animals
hours of sleep per day

Koala	Sloth	Armadillo	Opossum	Lemur
22	20	19	19	16

heaviest land mammal

African Elephant

Weighing in at up to 14,430 pounds (6,545 kg) and measuring approximately 24 feet (7.3 m) long, African elephants are truly humongous. Even at their great size, they are strictly vegetarian. They will, however, eat up to 500 pounds (226 kg) of vegetation a day! Their two tusks—which are actually elongated teeth—grow continuously during their lives and can reach about 9 feet (2.7 m) in length. Elephants live in small groups of 8 to 15 family members with one female (called a cow) as the leader.

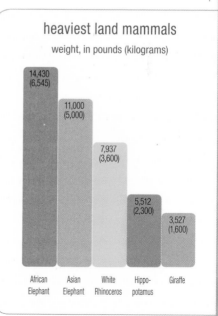

heaviest land mammals
weight, in pounds (kilograms)

Animal	Weight
African Elephant	14,430 (6,545)
Asian Elephant	11,000 (5,000)
White Rhinoceros	7,937 (3,600)
Hippopotamus	5,512 (2,300)
Giraffe	3,527 (1,600)

fastest land mammal

Cheetah

For short spurts, these sleek mammals can reach a speed of 71 miles (114 km) per hour. They can accelerate from 0 to 40 miles (64 km) per hour in just three strides. Their quickness easily enables these large African cats to outrun their prey. All other African cats can only stalk their prey because they lack the cheetah's amazing speed. Unlike the paws of all other cats, cheetah paws do not have skin sheaths (thin protective coverings). Their claws, therefore, cannot be retracted.

fastest land mammals

speed, in miles (kilometers) per hour

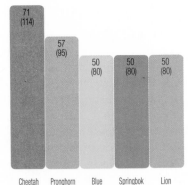

Cheetah	Pronghorn Antelope	Blue Wildebeest	Springbok	Lion
71 (114)	57 (95)	50 (80)	50 (80)	50 (80)

heaviest cat

Tiger

Although tigers average about 448 pounds (203 kg), some of these big cats can grow to 725 pounds (328 kg) and measure 6 feet (1.8 m) long—not including a 3-foot (0.9 m) tail. Tigers that live in colder habitats are usually larger than ones that live in warmer areas. These giant cats hunt at night, and can easily bring down a full-grown antelope alone. One tiger can eat about 60 pounds (27 kg) of meat in just one night. The five types of tigers are Bengal, Indochinese, South Chinese, Sumatran, and Siberian. All tiger species are endangered, mostly because of overhunting and loss of habitat due to farming and logging.

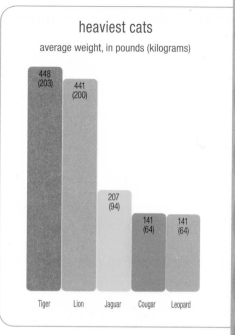

heaviest cats
average weight, in pounds (kilograms)

Tiger	Lion	Jaguar	Cougar	Leopard
448 (203)	441 (200)	207 (94)	141 (64)	141 (64)

largest rodent

Capybara

Capybaras reach an average length of 4 feet (1.2 m), stand about 20 inches (51 cm) tall, and weigh 75–150 pounds (34–68 kg)! That's about the same size as a Labrador retriever. Also known as water hogs and carpinchos, capybaras are found in South and Central America, where they spend much of their time in groups, looking for food. They are strictly vegetarian and have been known to raid gardens for melons and squash. Their partially webbed feet make capybaras excellent swimmers. They can dive down to the bottom of a lake or river to find plants and stay there for up to five minutes.

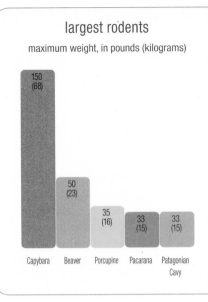

largest rodents

maximum weight, in pounds (kilograms)

Capybara	Beaver	Porcupine	Pacarana	Patagonian Cavy
150 (68)	50 (23)	35 (16)	33 (15)	33 (15)

animal with the longest teeth

African Elephant

An African elephant has two teeth that measure up to 118 inches (300 cm), or 9.8 feet (2.9 m) each. Also known as tusks, they are actually enlarged incisor teeth that are made of ivory. About 2 feet (0.6 m) of the tusk can be seen, and the rest reaches back and attaches to the skull. Both male and female African elephants have tusks, and they are mainly used for defense, digging, lifting, stripping tree bark, gathering food, and protecting the animal's sensitive trunk. While an elephant will grow six sets of molars, or chewing teeth, during its lifetime, it will only grow one set of tusks.

animals with the longest teeth

length in inches (cm)

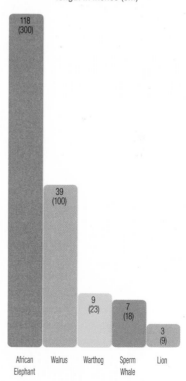

African Elephant	Walrus	Warthog	Sperm Whale	Lion
118 (300)	39 (100)	9 (23)	7 (18)	3 (9)

largest bat

Giant Flying Fox

The giant flying fox—a member of the megabat family—can have a wingspan of up to 6 feet (1.8 m). These furry mammals average just 7 wing beats per second, but can travel more than 40 miles (64 km) a night in search of food. Unlike smaller bats, which use echolocation, flying foxes rely on their acute vision and sense of smell to locate fruit, pollen, and nectar. Flying foxes got their name because their faces resemble a fox's face. Megabats live in the tropical areas of Africa, Asia, and Australia.

largest bats

wingspan, in feet (meters)

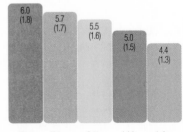

Giant Flying Fox	Malayan Flying Fox	Golden Crown	Lyle's Flying Fox	Indian Flying Fox
6.0 (1.8)	5.7 (1.7)	5.5 (1.6)	5.0 (1.5)	4.4 (1.3)

tallest land animal
Giraffe

Giraffes are the giants among mammals, growing up to 18 feet (5.5 m) in height. That means an average giraffe could look through the window of a two-story building! A giraffe's neck is 18 times longer than a human's, but both mammals have exactly the same number of neck bones. A giraffe's long legs enable it to outrun most of its enemies. When cornered, giraffes have the strength to kill a lion with a single kick to the head.

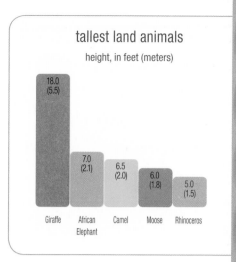

tallest land animals
height, in feet (meters)

18.0 (5.5)	7.0 (2.1)	6.5 (2.0)	6.0 (1.8)	5.0 (1.5)
Giraffe	African Elephant	Camel	Moose	Rhinoceros

largest domestic rabbit

Flemish Giant

The Flemish giant rabbit can weigh up to 20 pounds (9 kg) and measure about 2.5 feet (.7 m) long—about two and a half times the size of the average house cat. These rabbits are believed to have been first bred in Belgium in the 16th century, mostly for their meat and fur. In the early 20th century, Flemish giants became very popular in pet shows because of their large size and dense fur. The fur can be black, blue, fawn, light gray, sandy, steel gray, or white. Many Flemish giants are also owned as pets because they are very gentle animals. In captivity, they can live for up to ten years.

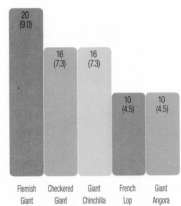

largest domestic rabbits

maximum weight in pounds (kilograms)

Flemish Giant	Checkered Giant	Giant Chinchilla	French Lop	Giant Angora
20 (9.0)	16 (7.3)	16 (7.3)	10 (4.5)	10 (4.5)

largest primate
Gorilla

Gorillas are the kings of the primate family, weighing in at up to 400 pounds (181 kg). The eastern lowland gorilla is the largest of the four subspecies of gorillas, which also include western lowland, Cross River, and mountain. All gorillas are found in Africa, and all but mountain gorillas live in tropical forests. They are mostly plant-eaters, but will occasionally eat small animals. An adult male gorilla can eat up to 45 pounds (32 kg) of food in a day. Gorillas live in groups of about 4 to 12 family members, and can live for about 35 years in the wild.

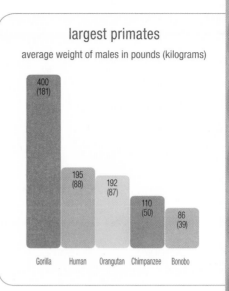

largest primates
average weight of males in pounds (kilograms)

Gorilla	400 (181)
Human	195 (88)
Orangutan	192 (87)
Chimpanzee	110 (50)
Bonobo	86 (39)

deadliest amphibian

Poison Dart Frog

Poison dart frogs are found mostly in the tropical rain forests of Central and South America, where they live on the moist land. These lethal amphibians have enough poison to kill up to 20 humans. A dart frog's poison is so effective that native Central and South Americans sometimes coat their hunting arrows or hunting darts with it. These brightly colored frogs can be yellow, orange, red, green, blue, or any combination of these colors. They measure only 0.5–2 inches (1–5 cm) long. There are approximately 75 different species of poison dart frogs.

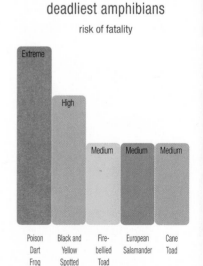

deadliest amphibians
risk of fatality

Extreme	High	Medium	Medium	Medium
Poison Dart Frog	Black and Yellow Spotted Frog	Fire-bellied Toad	European Salamander	Cane Toad

longest snake

Reticulated Python

Some adult reticulated pythons can grow to 27 feet (8.2 m) long, but most reach an average length of 17 feet (5 m). That's almost the length of an average school bus! These pythons live mostly in Asia, from Myanmar to Indonesia to the Philippines. Pythons have teeth that curl backward to hold their prey, and they hunt mainly at night for mammals and birds. Reticulated pythons are slow-moving creatures that kill their prey by constriction, or strangulation.

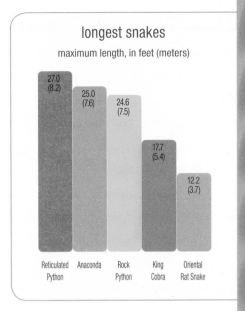

longest snakes
maximum length, in feet (meters)

Reticulated Python	Anaconda	Rock Python	King Cobra	Oriental Rat Snake
27.0 (8.2)	25.0 (7.6)	24.6 (7.5)	17.7 (5.4)	12.2 (3.7)

snake with the longest fangs
Gaboon Viper

The fangs of a Gaboon viper measure 2 inches (5.1 cm) in length! These giant fangs fold up against the snake's mouth so it does not pierce its own skin. When it is ready to strike its prey, the fangs snap down into position. The snake can grow up to 7 feet (2 m) long and weigh 18 pounds (8 kg). It is found in Africa and is perfectly camouflaged for hunting on the ground beneath leaves and grasses. The Gaboon viper's poison is not as toxic as some other snakes', but it is quite dangerous because of the amount of poison it can inject at one time. The snake is not very aggressive, however, and usually attacks only when bothered.

snakes with the longest fangs
fang length, in inches (centimeters)

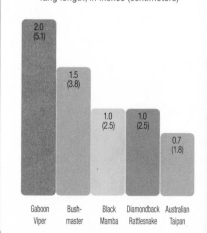

Gaboon Viper	Bush-master	Black Mamba	Diamondback Rattlesnake	Australian Taipan
2.0 (5.1)	1.5 (3.8)	1.0 (2.5)	1.0 (2.5)	0.7 (1.8)

country with the most reptile species

Australia

There are at least 987 reptile species living throughout the continent of Australia. Lizards account for the most with 737 species, followed by snakes with more than 200 different species. Australia also has more species of venomous snakes than any other continent. Among the deadliest Australian snakes are the common death adder, the lowlands copperhead, and several types of taipans. Many reptiles thrive in the hot, dry desert climate of Australia. The world's largest reptile—the saltwater crocodile—is also found there. Some of the other well-known reptile residents include sea and freshwater turtles, which nest and lay eggs along Australia's shoreline.

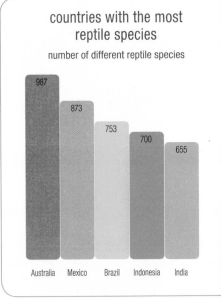

countries with the most reptile species
number of different reptile species

Australia	Mexico	Brazil	Indonesia	India
987	873	753	700	655

Australian frilled lizard

largest amphibian

Chinese Giant Salamander

With a length of 6 feet (1.8 m) and a weight of 55 pounds (25 kg), Chinese giant salamanders rule the amphibian world. This salamander has a large head, but its eyes and nostrils are small. It has short legs, a long tail, and very smooth skin. This large creature can be found in the streams of northeastern, central, and southern China. It feeds on fish, frogs, crabs, and snakes. The Chinese giant salamander will not hunt its prey. It waits until a potential meal wanders too close and then grabs it in its mouth. Because many people enjoy the taste of the salamander's meat, it is often hunted and its population is shrinking.

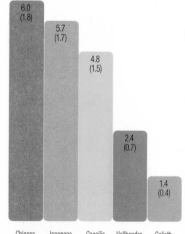

largest amphibians
maximum length, in feet (meters)

6.0 (1.8)	5.7 (1.7)	4.8 (1.5)	2.4 (0.7)	1.4 (0.4)
Chinese Giant Salamander	Japanese Giant Salamander	Caecilia Thompsoni	Hellbender	Goliath Frog

largest frog

Goliath Frog

The Goliath frog has a body that measures 13 inches (33 cm) long, but when its legs are extended, its total body length can increase to more than 2.5 feet (0.76 m). These gigantic frogs can weigh around 7 pounds (3 kg). Oddly enough, the eggs and tadpoles of this species are the same size as those of smaller frogs. Goliath frogs are found only in the western African countries of Equatorial Guinea and Cameroon. They live in rivers that are surrounded by dense rain forests. These huge amphibians are becoming endangered, mostly because their rain-forest homes are being destroyed.

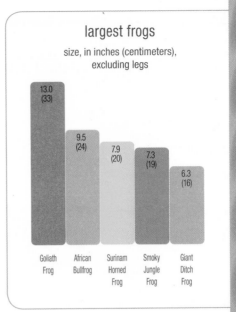

largest frogs
size, in inches (centimeters), excluding legs

Goliath Frog	13.0 (33)
African Bullfrog	9.5 (24)
Surinam Horned Frog	7.9 (20)
Smoky Jungle Frog	7.3 (19)
Giant Ditch Frog	6.3 (16)

largest lizard

Komodo Dragon

With a length of 10 feet (3 m) and a weight of 300 pounds (136 kg), Komodo dragons are the largest lizards roaming the earth. A Komodo dragon has a long neck and tail, and strong legs. These members of the monitor family are found mainly on Komodo Island, located in the Lesser Sunda Islands of Indonesia. Komodos are dangerous and have even been known to attack and kill humans. A Komodo uses its sense of smell to locate food, using its long, yellow tongue. A Komodo can consume 80 percent of its body weight in just one meal!

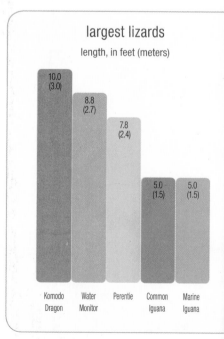

largest lizards
length, in feet (meters)

Komodo Dragon	Water Monitor	Perentie	Common Iguana	Marine Iguana
10.0 (3.0)	8.8 (2.7)	7.8 (2.4)	5.0 (1.5)	5.0 (1.5)

largest reptile

Saltwater Crocodile

Saltwater crocodiles can grow to 22 feet (6.7 m) long. That's about twice the length of the average car! However, males usually measure only about 17 feet (5 m) long, and females normally reach about 10 feet (3 m) in length. A large adult will feed on buffalo, monkeys, cattle, wild boar, and other large mammals. Saltwater crocodiles are found throughout the East Indies and Australia. Despite their name, saltwater crocodiles can also be found in freshwater and swamps. Some other common names for this species are the estuarine crocodile and the Indo-Pacific crocodile.

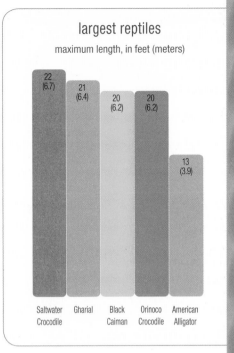

largest reptiles
maximum length, in feet (meters)

Saltwater Crocodile	Gharial	Black Caiman	Orinoco Crocodile	American Alligator
22 (6.7)	21 (6.4)	20 (6.2)	20 (6.2)	13 (3.9)

largest spider

Goliath Birdeater

A Goliath birdeater is about the same size as a dinner plate—it can grow to a total length of 11 inches (28 cm) and weigh about 6 ounces (170 g). A Goliath's spiderlings are also big—they can have a 6-inch (15 cm) leg span just one year after hatching. These giant tarantulas are found mostly in the rain forests of Guyana, Suriname, Brazil, and Venezuela. The Goliath birdeater's name is misleading— they commonly eat insects and small reptiles. Similar to other tarantula species, the Goliath birdeater lives in a burrow. The spider will wait by the opening to ambush prey that gets too close.

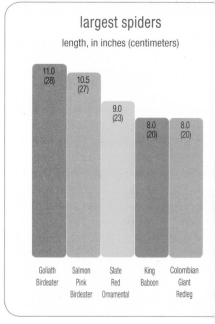

largest spiders

length, in inches (centimeters)

Goliath Birdeater	Salmon Pink Birdeater	Slate Red Ornamental	King Baboon	Colombian Giant Redleg
11.0 (28)	10.5 (27)	9.0 (23)	8.0 (20)	8.0 (20)

fastest-flying insect
Hawk Moth

The average hawk moth—which got its name from its swift and steady flight—can cruise along at speeds over 33 miles (53 km) per hour. That's faster than the average speed limit on most city streets! Although they are found throughout the world, most live in tropical climates. Also known as the sphinx moth and the hummingbird moth, this large insect can have a wingspan that reaches up to 8 inches (20 cm). Hawk moths also have good memories and may return to the same flowers at the same time each day.

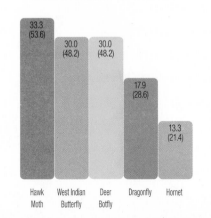

fastest-flying insects
speed, in miles (kilometers) per hour

Hawk Moth	West Indian Butterfly	Deer Botfly	Dragonfly	Hornet
33.3 (53.6)	30.0 (48.2)	30.0 (48.2)	17.9 (28.6)	13.3 (21.4)

163

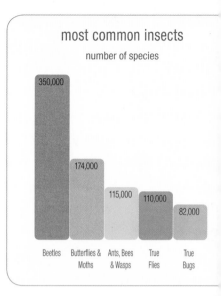

most common insect

Beetle

There are more than 350,000 different types of beetles crawling around in the world. Beetles make up about 25 percent of all types of life-forms on Earth, and about 40 percent of all insect species are beetles. They come in all shapes, colors, and sizes. The most common types of insects in this order are weevils and rove beetles. Some of the most well-known include ladybugs, fireflies, and dung beetles. Beetles are found in all climates except polar regions. Fossils indicate that beetles may have been around for about 300 million years.

most common insects
number of species

Beetles	Butterflies & Moths	Ants, Bees & Wasps	True Flies	True Bugs
350,000	174,000	115,000	110,000	82,000

longest insect migration

Monarch Butterfly

Millions of monarch butterflies travel to Mexico from all parts of North America every fall, flying as far as 2,700 miles (4,345 km). Once there, they will huddle together in the trees and wait out the cold weather. In spring and summer, most butterflies only live four or five weeks as adults, but in the fall, a special generation of monarchs is born. These butterflies will live for about seven months and participate in the great migration to Mexico. Scientists are studying these butterflies in the hope of learning how the insects know where and when to migrate to a place they have never visited before.

longest insect migrations

migration, in miles (kilometers)

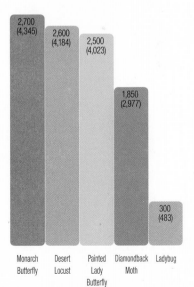

Monarch Butterfly	Desert Locust	Painted Lady Butterfly	Diamondback Moth	Ladybug
2,700 (4,345)	2,600 (4,184)	2,500 (4,023)	1,850 (2,977)	300 (483)

165

most common pet in the united states

Dog

More than 56.7 million households across the United States own one or more dogs. Approximately 83 million dogs live in the country. When it comes to finding a dog, approximately 21 percent of families head to a shelter to adopt one. Those who prefer purebreds tend to choose Labrador retrievers, German shepherds, and Yorkshire terriers. Some of the most popular dog names include Bella, Max, Daisy, and Buddy. In the United States, about 68 percent of households—or 82 million homes—own at least one type of pet.

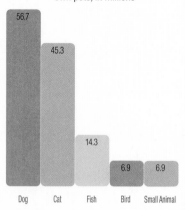

most common pets in the united states

number of US households that own pets, in millions

Dog	Cat	Fish	Bird	Small Animal
56.7	45.3	14.3	6.9	6.9

most popular dog breed in the united states

Labrador Retriever

Labrador retrievers are top dog in the United States! In 2012, the American Kennel Club recorded more purebred dog registrations for Labs than any other dog in the United States. Labs are very popular with families because of their gentle nature, and they are popular with hunters because of their retrieving skills. A very intelligent breed, Labrador retrievers can be trained to work in law enforcement or as guide dogs. They come in three colors—yellow, black, and brown—and are medium-size athletic dogs. They are considered by the American Kennel Club to be part of the sporting class.

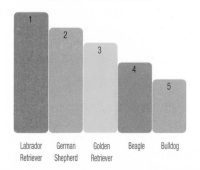

most popular dog breeds in the united states

american kennel club rank

1	2	3	4	5
Labrador Retriever	German Shepherd	Golden Retriever	Beagle	Bulldog

most popular cat breed in the united states

Persian

The Cat Fanciers' Association—the world's largest registry of pedigree cats—ranks the Persian as the most popular cat in the country. These flat-faced cats are known for their gentle personalities, which make them popular family pets. Persians come in many colors, including silver, golden, smoke, and tabby. They have long hair, which requires continuous grooming and maintenance. These pets, like most other cat breeds, can live as long as 15 years.

most popular cat breeds in the united states

cat fanciers' association rank

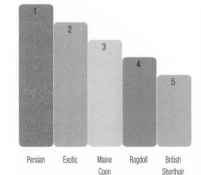

Persian	Exotic	Maine Coon	Ragdoll	British Shorthair
1	2	3	4	5

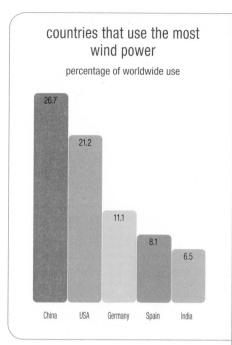

country that uses the most wind power

China

China produces 26.7 percent of the world's wind power. Wind is the country's third-largest energy source after coal and hydropower. There are about 480 wind farms in 29 of the country's 31 provinces. China has enough turbines to generate 61 gigawatts of power, which accounts for about 2 percent of the country's total energy. China plans to expand its wind turbines to increase its production by about 17 gigawatts each year. There are about 15 Chinese companies that produce wind turbines, and the three largest are Goldwind, Dongfang, and Sinovel.

countries that use the most wind power
percentage of worldwide use

Country	Percentage
China	26.7
USA	21.2
Germany	11.1
Spain	8.1
India	6.5

country with the most solar power

Germany

Germany generates about 32,411 megawatts of solar power each year—more than the next four countries combined. Solar power in Germany is slightly cheaper than traditional power sources, which have some of the highest rates in the world. Germany decommissioned its nuclear power plants in 2012 and turned to solar power plants. These plants now produce about 50 percent of the nation's power. Germany hopes to have 80 percent of its energy coming from solar plants by 2050. Solar power is much cleaner than fossil fuels, and therefore considered a "greener" option.

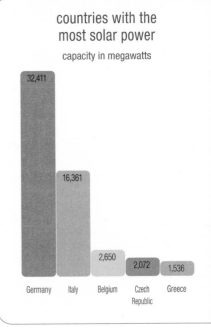

countries with the most solar power

capacity in megawatts

Germany	Italy	Belgium	Czech Republic	Greece
32,411	16,361	2,650	2,072	1,536

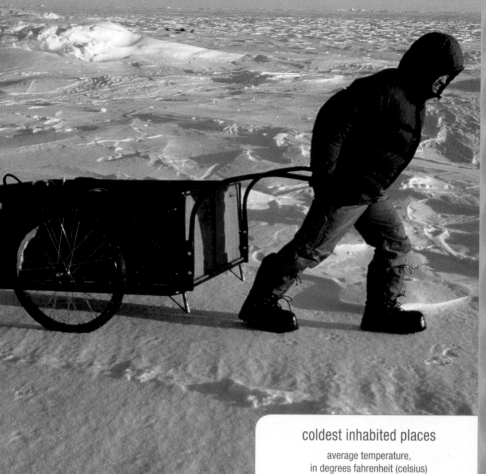

coldest inhabited place

Resolute

The residents of Resolute, Canada, have to bundle up—the average temperature is just -11.6°F (-24.2°C). Located on the northeast shore of Resolute Bay on the south coast of Cornwallis Island, the community is commonly the starting point for expeditions to the North Pole. In the winter it can stay dark for 24 hours, and in the summer it can stay light during the entire night. Only about 200 people brave the climate year-round, but the area is becoming quite popular with tourists.

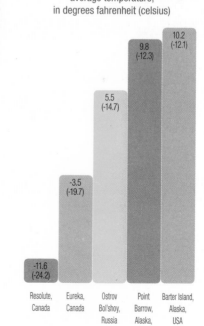

coldest inhabited places

average temperature,
in degrees fahrenheit (celsius)

Place	Temperature
Resolute, Canada	-11.6 (-24.2)
Eureka, Canada	-3.5 (-19.7)
Ostrov Bol'shoy, Russia	5.5 (-14.7)
Point Barrow, Alaska, USA	9.8 (-12.3)
Barter Island, Alaska, USA	10.2 (-12.1)

wettest inhabited place

Lloro

Umbrellas are in constant use in Lloro, Colombia, where the average annual rainfall totals about 524 inches (1,328 cm). That's about 1.4 inches (3.5 cm) a day, totaling more than 43 feet (13 m) a year! Located in the northwestern part of the country, Lloro is near the Pacific Ocean and the Caribbean Sea. Trade winds help bring lots of moisture from the coasts to this little tropical town, creating the humidity and precipitation that soak this lowland. Lloro is home to about 7,000 people.

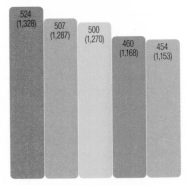

wettest inhabited places

average annual rainfall,
in inches (centimeters)

Lloro, Colombia	Puerto Lopez, Colombia	Mawsynram, India	Waialeale, Hawaii, USA	Cherrapunji, India
524 (1,328)	507 (1,287)	500 (1,270)	460 (1,168)	454 (1,153)

driest inhabited place

Aswan

Each year, only 0.02 inches (0.5 mm) of rain falls on Aswan, Egypt. In the country's sunniest and southernmost city, summer temperatures can reach a blistering 114°F (46°C). Aswan is located on the west bank of the Nile River, and it has a very busy marketplace that is also popular with tourists. The Aswan High Dam, at 12,565 feet (3,830 m) long, is the city's most famous landmark. It produces the majority of Egypt's power in the form of hydroelectricity.

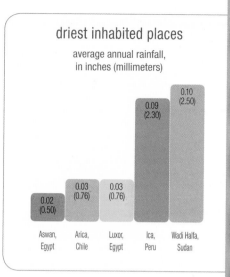

driest inhabited places

average annual rainfall, in inches (millimeters)

Aswan, Egypt	Arica, Chile	Luxor, Egypt	Ica, Peru	Wadi Halfa, Sudan
0.02 (0.50)	0.03 (0.76)	0.03 (0.76)	0.09 (2.30)	0.10 (2.50)

place with the fastest winds

Barrow Island

On April 12, 1996, Cyclone Olivia blew through Barrow Island in Australia and created a wind gust that reached 253 miles (407 km) an hour. Barrow Island is about 30 miles (48 km) off the coast of Western Australia and is home to many endangered species, such as dugongs and green turtles. The dry, sandy land measures about 78 square miles (202 sq km) and is the second-largest island in Western Australia. Barrow Island also has hundreds of oil wells and is a top source of oil for the country. The island has produced more than 300 million barrels of oil since 1967.

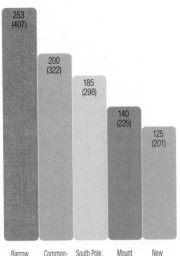

places with the fastest winds

speed of strongest winds,
in miles (kilometers) per hour

Place	Speed
Barrow Island, Australia	253 (407)
Commonwealth Bay, Antarctica	200 (322)
South Pole, Antarctica	185 (298)
Mount Washington, New Hampshire, USA	140 (225)
New Orleans, Louisiana, USA	125 (201)

hottest inhabited place
Dallol

Throughout the year, temperatures in Dallol, Ethiopia, average 93.2°F (34°C). Dallol is at the northernmost tip of the Great Rift Valley. The Dallol Depression reaches 328 feet (100 m) below sea level, making it the lowest point below sea level that is not covered by water. The area also has several active volcanoes. The only people to inhabit the region are the Afar, who have adapted to the harsh conditions there. For instance, to collect water, the women build covered stone piles and wait for condensation to form on the rocks.

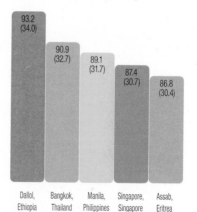

hottest inhabited places
average temperature, in degrees fahrenheit (celsius)

Dallol, Ethiopia	Bangkok, Thailand	Manila, Philippines	Singapore, Singapore	Assab, Eritrea
93.2 (34.0)	90.9 (32.7)	89.1 (31.7)	87.4 (30.7)	86.8 (30.4)

175

tallest tree

California Redwood

Growing in both California and southern Oregon, California redwoods can reach a height of 385 feet (117 m). Their trunks can grow up to 25 feet (8 m) in diameter. The tallest redwood on record is more than 60 feet (18 m) taller than the Statue of Liberty. Amazingly, this giant tree grows from a seed the size of a tomato. Some redwoods are believed to be more than 2,000 years old. The trees' thick bark and foliage protect them from natural hazards, such as insects and fires.

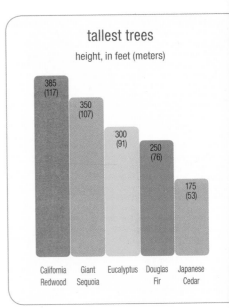

tallest trees
height, in feet (meters)

California Redwood	Giant Sequoia	Eucalyptus	Douglas Fir	Japanese Cedar
385 (117)	350 (107)	300 (91)	250 (76)	175 (53)

most poisonous mushroom
Death Cap

Death cap mushrooms are members of the Amanita family, which are among the most dangerous mushrooms in the world. The death cap contains deadly peptide toxins that cause rapid loss of bodily fluids and intense thirst. Within six hours, the poison shuts down the kidneys, liver, and central nervous system, causing coma and—in more than 50 percent of cases—death. Estimates of the number of poisonous mushroom species range from 80 to 2,000. Most experts agree, however, that at least 100 varieties will cause severe symptoms and even death if eaten.

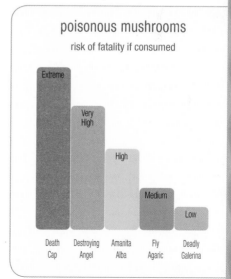

poisonous mushrooms
risk of fatality if consumed

Extreme	Very High	High	Medium	Low
Death Cap	Destroying Angel	Amanita Alba	Fly Agaric	Deadly Galerina

largest flower

Rafflesia

The blossoms of the giant rafflesia—or stinking corpse lily—can reach 36 inches (91 cm) in diameter and weigh up to 25 pounds (11 kg). Its petals can grow 1.5 feet (0.5 m) long and 1 inch (2.5 cm) thick. There are 16 different species of rafflesia. This endangered plant is found only in the rain forests of Borneo and Sumatra. It lives inside the bark of host vines and is noticeable only when its flowers break through to blossom. The large, reddish-purple flowers give off a smell similar to rotting meat, which attracts insects that help spread the rafflesia's pollen.

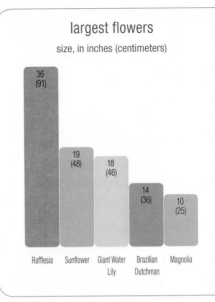

largest flowers
size, in inches (centimeters)

- Rafflesia 36 (91)
- Sunflower 19 (48)
- Giant Water Lily 18 (46)
- Brazilian Dutchman 14 (36)
- Magnolia 10 (25)

tallest cactus

Saguaro

Many saguaro cacti grow to a height of 50 feet (15 m), but some have actually reached 75 feet (23 m). That's taller than a seven-story building! Saguaros start out quite small and grow very slowly. A saguaro reaches only about 1 inch (2.5 cm) high during its first 10 years. It will not bloom until it is between 50 and 75 years old. By this time, the cactus has a strong root system that can support about 9–10 tons (8–9 t) of growth. Its spines can measure up to 2.5 inches (5 cm) long. Saguaro cacti live for about 170 years. The giant cacti can be found from southeastern California to southern Arizona.

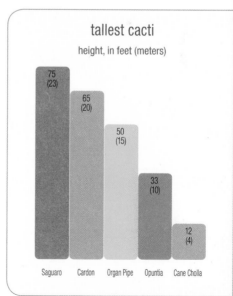

tallest cacti
height, in feet (meters)

Saguaro	75 (23)
Cardon	65 (20)
Organ Pipe	50 (15)
Opuntia	33 (10)
Cane Cholla	12 (4)

most intense earthquake since 1900

Chile

An explosive earthquake measuring 9.5 on the Richter scale rocked the coast of Chile on May 22, 1960. This is equal to the intensity of about 60,000 hydrogen bombs. Some 2,000 people were killed and another 3,000 injured. The death toll was fairly low because the foreshocks frightened people into the streets. When the massive jolt came, many of the buildings that collapsed were already empty. The coastal towns of Valdivia and Puerto Montt suffered the most damage because they were closest to the epicenter—located about 100 miles (161 km) offshore. On February 27, 2010, Chile was rocked by another huge earthquake (8.8 magnitude), but the loss of life and property was much less than from previous quakes.

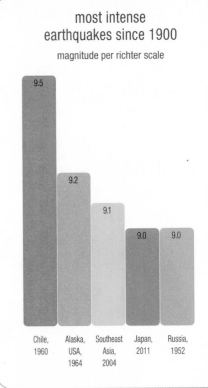

most intense earthquakes since 1900
magnitude per richter scale

Chile, 1960	Alaska, USA, 1964	Southeast Asia, 2004	Japan, 2011	Russia, 1952
9.5	9.2	9.1	9.0	9.0

most destructive flood since 1900

Hurricane Katrina

The pounding rain and storm surges of Hurricane Katrina resulted in catastrophic flooding that cost about $60 billion. The storm formed in late August 2005 over the Bahamas, moved across Florida, and finally hit Louisiana on August 29 as a category-3 storm. The storm surge from the Gulf of Mexico flooded the state, as well as neighboring Alabama and Mississippi. Many levees could not hold back the massive amounts of water, and entire towns were destroyed. In total, some 1,800 people lost their lives.

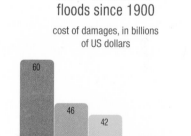

most destructive floods since 1900

cost of damages, in billions of US dollars

60	46	42	30	27

| Hurricane Katrina, USA, 2005 | Chao Phraya River, Thailand, 2011 | Hurricane Sandy, USA, 2012 | Yangtze River, China, 1998 | Bangladesh, 1970 |

worst oil spill

Gulf War

During the Gulf War in 1991, Iraqi troops opened valves of oil wells in Kuwait, releasing more than 240 million gallons (908 million L) of oil into the Persian Gulf. At its worst, the spill measured 101 miles by 42 miles (163 km by 68 km) and was about 5 inches (13 cm) thick. Some of the oil eventually evaporated, another 1 million barrels were collected out of the water, and the rest washed ashore. Although much of the oil can no longer be seen, most of it remains, soaked into the deeper layers of sand along the coast. Amazingly, the wildlife that lives in these areas were not immediately harmed as much as was initially feared. However, salt marsh areas without strong currents were hit the hardest, as oil collected there and killed off entire ecosystems.

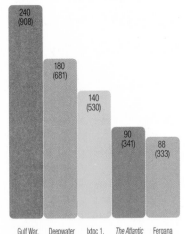

worst oil spills
oil spilled, in millions of gallons (liters)

Gulf War, Kuwait, 1991	Deepwater Horizon, USA, 2010	Ixtoc 1, Mexico, 1979	The Atlantic Empress/ Aegean Captain, Trinidad & Tobago, 1979	Fergana Valley, Uzbekistan, 1992
240 (908)	180 (681)	140 (530)	90 (341)	88 (333)

most destructive tornado since 1900

Joplin, Missouri

On May 22, 2011, a category EF5 tornado ripped through Joplin, Missouri, and destroyed about 2,000 buildings, or 25 percent, of the small Midwest town. The devastating storm caused damage totaling $2.8 billion and killed 161 people. The tornado measured up to a mile (1.6 km) wide, and was part of a large outbreak of storms during that week, which affected Arkansas, Kansas, and Oklahoma. A category-5 tornado on the Enhanced Fujita (EF) scale is the most intense, capable of producing winds greater than 200 miles (322 km) per hour. With more than 1,000 storms popping up across the country, 2011 was the deadliest year for tornadoes in fifty years.

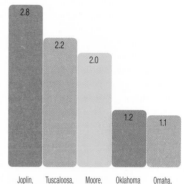

most destructive
tornadoes since 1900

cost of damages, in billions
of US dollars

Joplin, Missouri, 2011	Tuscaloosa, Alabama, 2011	Moore, Oklahoma, 2013	Oklahoma City, Oklahoma, 1999	Omaha, Nebraska, 1975
2.8	2.2	2.0	1.2	1.1

world's most intense hurricane since 1900

Super Typhoon Haiyan

With winds reaching a top speed of 195 miles per hour (314 kph), Super Typhoon Haiyan was the most intense hurricane in the last 115 years. The category-5 storm, also known as Typhoon Yolanda, made landfall in the Philippines on November 8, 2013. The raging storm destroyed more than 600,000 people's homes, and caused $14 billion in damage. More than 6,200 people lost their lives. The most devastating effect of the typhoon was from the storm surge that caused widespread flooding. Regions of Micronesia, Palau, southern China, and Vietnam were also affected.

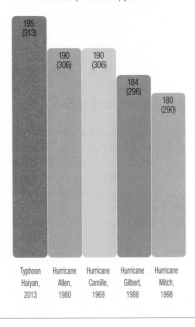

world's most intense hurricanes since 1900

highest sustained wind speeds, in miles (kilometers) per hour

195 (313)	190 (306)	190 (306)	184 (296)	180 (290)
Typhoon Haiyan, 2013	Hurricane Allen, 1980	Hurricane Camille, 1969	Hurricane Gilbert, 1988	Hurricane Mitch, 1998

highest tsunami wave since 1900

Lituya Bay

A 1,720-foot (524 m) tsunami wave crashed down in Lituya Bay, Alaska, on July 9, 1958. Located in Glacier Bay National Park, the tsunami was caused by a massive landslide that was triggered by an 8.3-magnitude earthquake. The water from the bay covered 5 square miles (13 sq km) of land and traveled inland as far as 3,600 feet (1,097 m). Millions of trees were washed away. Amazingly, because the area was very isolated and the coastline was sheltered by coves, only two people died when their fishing boat sank.

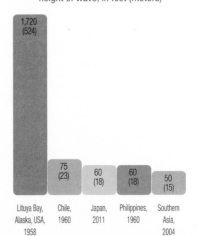

highest tsunami waves since 1900

height of wave, in feet (meters)

Lituya Bay, Alaska, USA, 1958	Chile, 1960	Japan, 2011	Philippines, 1960	Southern Asia, 2004
1,720 (524)	75 (23)	60 (18)	60 (18)	50 (15)

Size Wise

The state of Rhode Island can fit inside the state of Alaska 488 times. However, the population of Rhode Island is more than 30 percent larger than Alaska's population. Alaska's capital city, Juneau, is about 3,000 square miles (7,770 km), which is larger than the state of Delaware.

Juneau, Alaska

Tinsel Towns

There are three towns in the US that are called Santa Claus. In Santa Claus, Indiana, many residents live in the gated community of Christmas Lake Village. Santa Claus, Georgia, features streets including Candy Cane Road, Rudolph Way, and Sleigh Street. Santa Claus, Arizona, is a tiny town in the Mohave Desert with few inhabitants left.

Seeing Red

The Northern cardinal is the most common state bird in the US, with seven states claiming it as an official symbol. These states are Illinois, Indiana, Kentucky, North Carolina, Ohio, Virginia, and West Virginia. The western meadowlark comes in second with six states.

Big Bay

There are more than 100 main estuaries—bodies of water with a mix of salt and fresh water—in the United States, and the largest is the Chesapeake Bay between Maryland and Virginia. It stretches for about 200 miles (321 km) and holds 18 trillion gallons (68 trillion) of water. It is surprisingly shallow, and more than 700,000 acres (283,279 ha) are less than 6 feet (1.8 m) deep.

National Treasure Trips

In 1872, Yellowstone was established as the world's first National Park. Since then, the National Park System has grown to include 401 parks, monuments, battlefields, historic sites, seashores, and recreation areas. These cover more than 84 million acres (33.9 million ha) across all states and US territories. California and Alaska have the most National Parks with 8 each.

Got that Straight?

The longest straight road in the United States is North Dakota Highway 46. The road stretches for 123 miles (198 km) along the prairies, and the straightest section runs between Gackle and Beaver Creek. Although the road makes a few slight veers to the left or right, there are absolutely no curves or turns.

Tremendous Tunnels

There are thousands of caves that run through the United States, and most are made from limestone. It takes between 10,000 to 100,000 years to create a cave that's large enough for human exploration. The largest cave in the country is Mammoth Cave in Kentucky, which has more than 300 miles (482 km) of tunnels and passageways.

state with the oldest mardi gras celebration

Alabama

People in Mobile, Alabama, have been celebrating Mardi Gras since 1703, although they did not have an official parade event until 1831. After a brief hiatus during the Civil War, the celebrations started back up in 1866 and have been growing ever since. Today, some 100,000 people gather in Mobile to enjoy the 40 parades that take place during the two weeks that lead up to Mardi Gras. On the biggest day—Fat Tuesday—six parades wind through the downtown waterfront, with floats and costumed dancers. But at the stroke of midnight, the partying stops and plans for the next year begin.

united states' oldest mardi gras celebrations

number of years since celebration began*

183	179	172	170	147
Mobile, Alabama (1831)	New Orleans, Louisiana (1835)	Lafayette, Louisiana (1842)	Pensacola, Florida (1844)	Galveston, Texas (1867)

*As of 2014

state with the largest national forest

Alaska

The Tongass National Forest covers approximately 16,800,000 acres (6,798,900 ha) in southeast Alaska. That's about the same size as West Virginia. It is also home to the world's largest temperate rain forest. Some of the forest's trees are more than 700 years old. About 11,000 miles (17,703 km) of shoreline are inside the park. Some of the animals that live in the forest include bears, salmon, and wolves. The world's largest group of bald eagles also spends the fall and winter here on the Chilkat River.

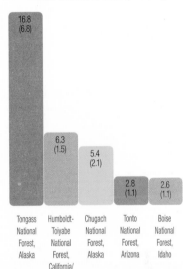

united states' largest national forests

size, in millions of acres (hectares)

Forest	Size
Tongass National Forest, Alaska	16.8 (6.8)
Humboldt-Toiyabe National Forest, California/Nevada	6.3 (1.5)
Chugach National Forest, Alaska	5.4 (2.1)
Tonto National Forest, Arizona	2.8 (1.1)
Boise National Forest, Idaho	2.6 (1.1)

state with the largest collection of telescopes

Arizona

The Kitt Peak National Observatory is home to 27 different telescopes—25 optical telescopes and 2 radio telescopes. Located above the Sonora Desert, the site was chosen to house the collection of equipment because of its clear weather, low relative humidity, and steady atmosphere. Eight different astronomical research institutions maintain and operate the telescopes. The observatory is overseen by the National Optical Astronomy Observatories. One of the most prominent telescopes at Kitt Peak is the McMath-Pierce Solar Telescope, the second-largest solar telescope in the world.

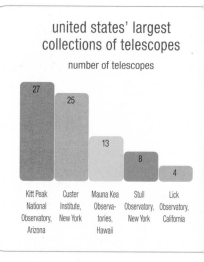

united states' largest collections of telescopes

number of telescopes

Kitt Peak National Observatory, Arizona	27
Custer Institute, New York	25
Mauna Kea Observatories, Hawaii	13
Stull Observatory, New York	8
Lick Observatory, California	4

state that grows the most rice

Arkansas

Farmers in Arkansas produced 4.04 million tons (3.6 million t) of rice in 2013, which was more than 43 percent of all rice grown in the country. With that harvest, farmers could give every person in the United States 25 pounds (11 kg) of rice and still have a little left over. There are more than 1.19 million acres (484,004 ha) of rice planted across Arkansas. Agriculture is a very important part of the state's economy, employing more than 287,000 workers, or about 20 percent of the state's workforce.

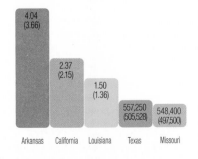

states that grow
the most rice

production in 2013, in millions
of tons (metric tons)

Arkansas	4.04 (3.66)
California	2.37 (2.15)
Louisiana	1.50 (1.36)
Texas	557,250 (505,528)
Missouri	548,400 (497,500)

state with the most-visited national site

California

More than 14.3 million people visited the Golden Gate National Recreation Area in California during 2013. The park, which stretches for about 60 miles (96 km) around the San Francisco Bay area, is one of the world's largest urban national parks at more than 80,000 acres (32,375 ha). Some of the most well-known tourist spots in the park include Muir Woods National Monument, Alcatraz, and the Presidio of San Francisco. Visitors can jog, windsurf, hike, hang glide, picnic, or simply enjoy the breathtaking views. There are about 1,200 different plant and animal species living in the Golden Gate National Recreation area.

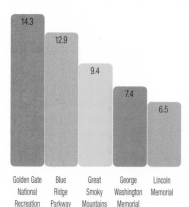

united states' most-visited national sites

annual attendance, in millions

Site	Attendance
Golden Gate National Recreation Area	14.3
Blue Ridge Parkway	12.9
Great Smoky Mountains National Park	9.4
George Washington Memorial Parkway	7.4
Lincoln Memorial	6.5

state with the tallest sand dunes
Colorado

Star Dune, located in Great Sand Dunes National Park near Mosca, Colorado, is 750 feet (229 m) tall. That's almost five times taller than the Statue of Liberty! The park's dunes were formed from sand left behind by evaporated lakes. Wind picked up the sand and funneled it through the surrounding mountains until it collected in this low-lying region. Visitors to the park are allowed to ski, sled, or slide down the giant dunes; this works best after a light rain. Many animals also call this park home, including pika, marmots, black bears, and mountain lions.

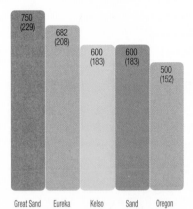

united states' tallest sand dunes

height, in feet (meters)

750 (229)	682 (208)	600 (183)	600 (183)	500 (152)
Great Sand Dunes, Colorado	Eureka Dunes, California	Kelso Dunes, California	Sand Mountain, Nevada	Oregon Dunes, California

state with the oldest amusement park

Connecticut

Lake Compounce in Bristol, Connecticut, first opened as a picnic park in 1846. The park's first electric roller coaster, the Green Dragon, was introduced in 1914 and cost ten cents per ride. It was replaced by the Wildcat in 1927, and the wooden coaster still operates today. In 1996 the park got a $50 million upgrade, which included the thrilling new roller coaster Boulder Dash. It is the only coaster to be built into a mountainside. Another $3.3 million was spent on upgrades in 2005, including an 800-foot (244 m) lazy river.

196

united states' oldest amusement parks

number of years open*

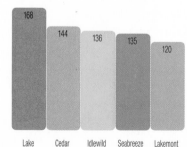

Lake Compounce, Connecticut (1846)	Cedar Point, Ohio (1870)	Idlewild Park, Pennsylvania (1878)	Seabreeze Park, New York (1879)	Lakemont Park, Pennsylvania (1894)
168	144	136	135	120

*As of 2014

state with the oldest church

Delaware

Old Swedes Church in Wilmington, Delaware, was built in 1699. First established as a Swedish Lutheran church, it is the nation's oldest church building still standing in its original form. The church's cemetery, a plot that was first used in 1638, is believed to hold many of Delaware's first settlers. In fact, when the church was first constructed near the cemetery, the foundation was built around a number of early plots, giving it an unusual shape. Old Swedes Church was designated as a National Historic Landmark in 1963.

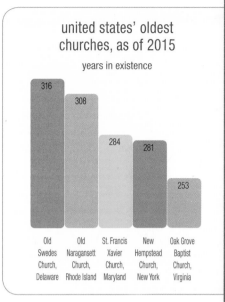

united states' oldest churches, as of 2015

years in existence

Old Swedes Church, Delaware	Old Naragansett Church, Rhode Island	St. Francis Xavier Church, Maryland	New Hempstead Church, New York	Oak Grove Baptist Church, Virginia
316	308	284	281	253

state with the most lightning strikes

Florida

Southern Florida is known as the Lightning Capital of the United States, with 24.7 bolts occurring over each square mile (2.6 sq km)—the equivalent of ten city blocks—each year. Some 70 percent of all strikes occur between noon and 6:00 p.m., and the most dangerous months are July and August. Most lightning bolts measure 2 to 3 miles (5.2 to 7.8 km) long and can generate between 100 million and 1 billion volts of electricity. The air in a lightning bolt is heated to 50,000°F (27,760°C).

states with the most lightning strikes

annual bolts per square mile (2.6 sq km)

Florida	Louisiana	Mississippi	Alabama	Arkansas
24.7	19.7	18.4	16.0	15.2

state with the largest sports hall of fame

Georgia

The Georgia Sports Hall of Fame fills 43,000 square feet (3,995 sq m) with memorabilia from Georgia's most accomplished college, amateur, and professional athletes. Some 230,000 bricks, 245 tons (222 t) of steel, and 7,591 pounds (3,443 kg) of glass were used in its construction. The hall owns more than 3,000 artifacts and displays about 1,000 of them at a time. Some Hall of Famers include baseball legend Hank Aaron, Olympic basketball great Theresa Edwards, and Super Bowl I champion Bill Curry.

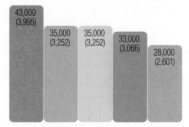

united states' largest sports halls of fame

area, in square feet (square meters)

Georgia Sports Hall of Fame	Virginia Sports Hall of Fame	Texas Sports Hall of Fame	Alabama Sports Hall of Fame	Louisiana Sports Hall of Fame
43,000 (3,995)	35,000 (3,252)	35,000 (3,252)	33,000 (3,066)	28,000 (2,601)

199

state with the world's largest submillimeter wavelength telescope

Hawaii

Mauna Kea—located on the island of Hawaii—is home to the world's largest submillimeter wavelength telescope, with a diameter of 49 feet (15 m). The James Clerk Maxwell Telescope (JCMT) is used to study our solar system, interstellar dust and gas, and distant galaxies. Mauna Kea also houses one of the world's largest optical/infrared (Keck I and II) and dedicated infrared (UKIRT) telescopes in the world. Mauna Kea is an ideal spot for astronomy because the atmosphere above the dormant volcano is very dry with little cloud cover, and its distance from city lights ensures a clear night sky.

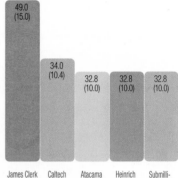

world's largest submillimeter wavelength telescopes

diameter of lens, in feet (meters)

James Clerk Maxwell Telescope (JCMT), Hawaii, USA	Caltech Submillimeter Observatory (CSO), Hawaii, USA	Atacama Submillimeter Telescope (ASTE), Chile	Heinrich Hertz Telescope (HHT), Arizona, USA	Submillimeter Telescope (SMT), Arizona, USA
49.0 (15.0)	34.0 (10.4)	32.8 (10.0)	32.8 (10.0)	32.8 (10.0)

state that harvests the most farm-raised trout

Idaho

Idaho topped farm-raised trout sales in 2013 with a total of $44.3 million—about 46 percent of the total trout sales in the United States. Trout farmers in the state sold about 30 million fish with a combined weight of 35.5 million pounds (16.1 million k). That's enough fish to feed everyone in the state a meal per week for a year. There are about 115 aquaculture facilities in the state. About 98 percent of aquaculture production takes place along the Snake River in Gooding, Twin Falls, and Jerome counties. Fish hatcheries first opened in Idaho in the 1930s.

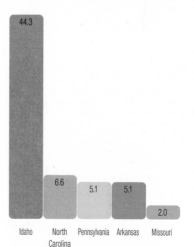

states that harvest the
most farm-raised trout

sales in 2013, in millions of US dollars

State	Sales
Idaho	44.3
North Carolina	6.6
Pennsylvania	5.1
Arkansas	5.1
Missouri	2.0

201

state with the largest public college library

Illinois

The library at the University of Illinois at Urbana-Champaign has more than 10.5 million books on its shelves. The student body is made up of approximately 32,200 undergraduates and 12,200 graduate students. If each of these students checked out 235 books, there would still be some left in the library. The most popular majors at the school include finance, engineering, and social sciences. The University of Illinois at Urbana-Champaign is situated on a 1,783-acre (721.5 ha) campus, and is located about 130 miles (209.2 km) south of Chicago.

states with the largest public college library
number of volumes, in millions

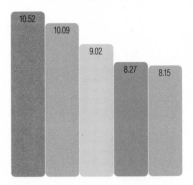

University of Illinois at Urbana-Champaign	University of California, Berkeley	University of Texas at Austin	University of Michigan—Ann Arbor	University of California—Los Angeles
10.52	10.09	9.02	8.27	8.15

state with the largest half marathon

Indiana

Cars aren't the only things racing in Indianapolis, Indiana. Each May some 35,000 runners take part in the OneAmerica 500 Festival Mini-Marathon. This makes the Mini-Marathon the nation's largest half marathon and the nation's eighth-longest road race. The 13.1-mile (21.1 km) race winds through downtown and includes a lap along the Indianapolis Motor Speedway oval. A giant pasta dinner and after-race party await the runners at the end of the day. The Mini-Marathon is part of a weekend celebration that centers around the Indianapolis 500 auto race.

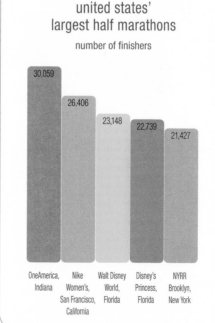

united states' largest half marathons

number of finishers

Race	Finishers
OneAmerica, Indiana	30,059
Nike Women's, San Francisco, California	26,406
Walt Disney World, Florida	23,148
Disney's Princess, Florida	22,739
NYRR Brooklyn, New York	21,427

203

state with the highest egg production

Iowa

Iowa tops all other states in the country in egg production, turning out almost 14.8 billion eggs per year. That's enough to give every person in the United States about three and a half dozen eggs each! That's a good thing, because each person in America eats about 248 eggs per year. The state has 53 million laying hens, and each is capable of laying about 279 eggs a year. These hungry hens eat about 57 million bushels of corn and 28.5 million bushels of soybeans annually. In addition to selling the eggs as they are, Iowa's processing plants turn them into frozen, liquid, dried, or specialty egg products.

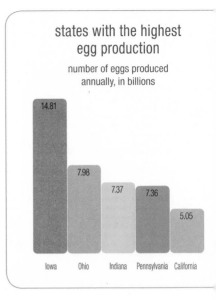

states with the highest egg production

number of eggs produced annually, in billions

Iowa	Ohio	Indiana	Pennsylvania	California
14.81	7.98	7.37	7.36	5.05

state with the windiest city
Kansas

According to average annual wind speeds collected by the National Climatic Data Center, Dodge City, Kansas, is the windiest city in the United States, with an average wind speed of 13.9 miles (22.3 km) per hour. Located in Ford County, the city borders the Santa Fe Trail and is rich in history. The city was founded in 1872 and had a reputation as a tough cowboy town. With help from legendary sheriffs like Wyatt Earp, order was established and the town grew steadily. Today, tourists come to learn about the area's history.

united states' windiest cities
average wind speed, in miles (kilometers) per hour

City	Average wind speed
Dodge City, Kansas	13.9 (22.3)
Amarillo, Texas	13.5 (21.7)
Cheyenne, Wyoming	12.9 (20.7)
Rochester, Minnesota	12.8 (20.6)
Kahului, Hawaii	12.8 (20.6)

state with the most popular horse race

Kentucky

Each year, the Kentucky Derby draws more than 151,000 people who gather to watch "the most exciting two minutes in sports." The race is run at Churchill Downs in Louisville, on a dirt track that measures 1.25 miles (2 km) long. The thoroughbred horses must be three years old to race, and the winner nabs a $2 million purse. The winning horse is covered in a blanket of 554 red roses, which gave the race the nickname "The Run for the Roses." The fastest horse to complete the race was Secretariat in 1973, with a time of 1:59:40.

united states' most popular horse races

attendance in 2013

Kentucky Derby, Kentucky	Preakness, Maryland	Breeders' Cup, California	Carolina Cup, South Carolina	Belmont Stakes, New York
151,616	117,203	94,628	65,000	47,562

Secretariat

state with the tallest capitol building

Louisiana

The Louisiana State Capitol rises 460 feet (140.2 m) above Baton Rouge. The 34-story building is the tallest in the city, and the seventh-tallest building in the state. It is home to the Louisiana State Legislature, and the governor's and lieutenant governor's offices. Opened to the public in May 1932, the Louisiana State Capitol took 29 months to complete and cost $5 million. The art deco building's main tower includes sculptures that depict important events in Louisiana's history. The Capitol Gardens are on the surrounding 30 acres (12 ha), and 10 miles (16.1 km) of sidewalks wind through the grounds. The building is a National Historic Landmark.

states with the tallest capitol buildings

height in feet (meters)

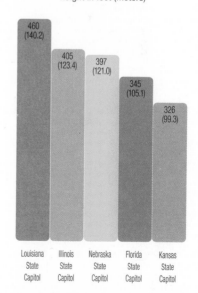

Louisiana State Capitol	Illinois State Capitol	Nebraska State Capitol	Florida State Capitol	Kansas State Capitol
460 (140.2)	405 (123.4)	397 (121.0)	345 (105.1)	326 (99.3)

state with the oldest state fair

Maine

The first Skowhegan State Fair was held in 1819—a year before Maine officially became a state! The fair took place in January, and hundreds of people came despite harsh weather. Originally sponsored by the Somerset Central Agricultural Society, the fair name became official in 1842. State fairs were very important in the 1800s. With no agricultural colleges in existence, fairs became the best way for farmers to learn about new agricultural methods and equipment. Today, the Skowhegan State Fair features more than 7,000 exhibitors who compete for prize money totaling more than $200,000. The fair also includes a demolition derby, a children's barnyard, concerts, livestock exhibits, and arts and crafts.

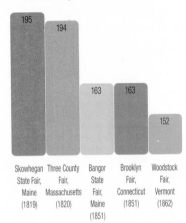

united states' oldest state fairs

number of years since fair first held*

Skowhegan State Fair, Maine (1819)	Three County Fair, Massachusetts (1820)	Bangor State Fair, Maine (1851)	Brooklyn Fair, Connecticut (1851)	Woodstock Fair, Vermont (1862)
195	194	163	163	152

*As of 2014

College Park Aviation Museum

state with the oldest airport
Maryland

The Wright brothers founded College Park Airport in 1909 to teach army officers how to fly, and it has been in operation ever since. The airport is now owned by the Maryland-National Capital Park and Planning Commission and is on the Register of Historic Places. Many aviation "firsts" occurred at this airport, such as the first woman passenger in the United States (1909), the first test of a bomb-dropping device (1911), and the first US airmail service (1918). The College Park Aviation Museum is located on its grounds, and it exhibits aviation memorabilia.

united states' oldest airports
number of years open*

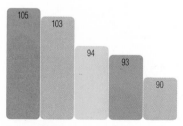

College Park Airport, Maryland (1909)	Robertson Airport, Connecticut (1911)	Hartness State Airport, Vermont (1920)	Middlesboro-Bell County Airport, Kentucky (1921)	Page Field, Florida (1924)
105	103	94	93	90

*As of 2014

209

state with the oldest baseball stadium

Massachusetts

Fenway Park opened its doors to Massachusetts baseball fans on April 20, 1912. The Boston Red Sox—the park's home team—won the World Series that year. The crowd celebrated in 2004 when the Sox won the World Series again. The park is also the home of the Green Monster—a giant 37-foot (11.3 m) wall with an additional 23-foot (7 m) screen that has plagued home-run hitters since the park first opened. The park's unique dimensions were not intended to prevent home runs, however; they were meant to keep nonpaying fans outside. A seat out in the right-field bleachers is painted red to mark where the longest measurable home run hit inside the park landed. It measured 502 feet (153 m) and was hit by Ted Williams in 1946. Some of the other baseball legends who played at Fenway include Cy Young, Babe Ruth, Jimmie Fox, and Carlton Fisk.

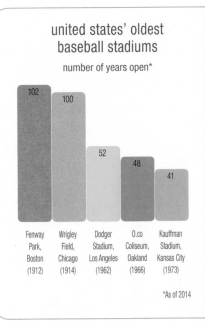

united states' oldest baseball stadiums

number of years open*

Stadium	Years
Fenway Park, Boston (1912)	102
Wrigley Field, Chicago (1914)	100
Dodger Stadium, Los Angeles (1962)	52
O.co Coliseum, Oakland (1966)	48
Kauffman Stadium, Kansas City (1973)	41

*As of 2014

BOSTON RED SOX

state with the largest stadium
Michigan

Michigan Stadium—also known as the Big House—is the home of the University of Michigan Wolverines, and can hold 109,901 football fans during the home games. The stadium was constructed in 1927 using 440 tons (399 t) of reinforcing steel and 31,000 square feet (2,880 sq m) of wire mesh to create an 82,000-seat venue. After several renovations, the stadium reached its current seating capacity in 2010. The most recent additions include luxury boxes and club seating. Since its inaugural game, Michigan Stadium has hosted more than 35 million fans.

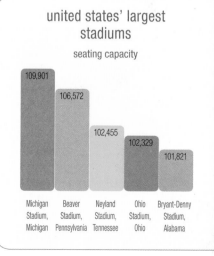

united states' largest stadiums
seating capacity

109,901	106,572	102,455	102,329	101,821
Michigan Stadium, Michigan	Beaver Stadium, Pennsylvania	Neyland Stadium, Tennessee	Ohio Stadium, Ohio	Bryant-Denny Stadium, Alabama

state with the largest indoor amusement park

Minnesota

Nickelodeon Universe is located inside the Mall of America in Bloomington, Minnesota, and covers 7 acres (2.8 ha). The park offers more than 20 rides, including the SpongeBob SquarePants Rock Bottom Plunge, Splat-O-Sphere, Teenage Mutant Ninja Turtles Shell Shock, Log Chute, the Fairly Odd Coaster, and Avatar Airbender. Some of the other attractions at the park are a rock-climbing wall, petting zoo, and game arcade. Kids can also meet Dora, Diego, Patrick, and SpongeBob.

united states' largest indoor amusement parks
area, in acres (hectares)

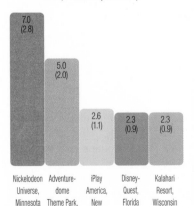

Park	Area
Nickelodeon Universe, Minnesota	7.0 (2.8)
Adventuredome Theme Park, Nevada	5.0 (2.0)
iPlay America, New Jersey	2.6 (1.1)
Disney-Quest, Florida	2.3 (0.9)
Kalahari Resort, Wisconsin	2.3 (0.9)

state with the most catfish
Mississippi

Mississippi sold more than $184 million in catfish in 2013. There are about 388 million catfish in Mississippi—more than 60 percent of the world's farm-raised supply. That's almost enough to give every person in the state about 132 fish each. There are about 48,600 water acres (19,425 ha) used to farm catfish in Mississippi. The state's residents are quite proud of their successful fish industry and celebrate at the World Catfish Festival in Belzoni.

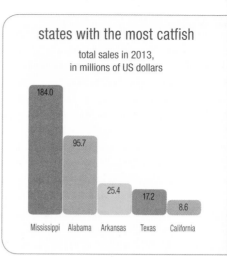

states with the most catfish
total sales in 2013, in millions of US dollars

Mississippi	Alabama	Arkansas	Texas	California
184.0	95.7	25.4	17.2	8.6

state with the largest outdoor theater

Missouri

The Municipal Theatre in St. Louis, Missouri—affectionately known as the Muny—is the nation's largest outdoor theater, with 80,000 square feet (7,432 sq m) and 11,500 seats—about the same size as a regulation soccer field. Amazingly, construction for the giant theater was completed in just 42 days at a cost of $10,000. The theater opened in 1917 with a production of Verdi's *Aïda*, and the best seats cost only $1. The Muny offers classic Broadway shows each summer, with past productions including *The King and I*, *The Wizard of Oz*, and *Oliver!* The last nine rows of the theater are always held as free seats for the public, just as they have been since the Muny opened.

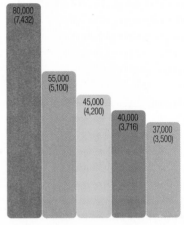

united states' largest outdoor theaters

area, in square feet (square meters)

Theater	Area
Municipal Theatre, Missouri	80,000 (7,432)
Alpine Valley Music Theatre, Wisconsin	55,000 (5,100)
The Pavilion, New Mexico	45,000 (4,200)
Henderson Pavilion, Nevada	40,000 (3,716)
Miller Outdoor Theater, Texas	37,000 (3,500)

state with the largest ski resort

Montana

If the ski trails at Big Sky Resort in Montana were combined, they would stretch more than 155 miles (250 km)! Operating 22 chair lifts and 7 surface lifts, Big Sky can handle 29,000 skiers per hour on its 5,750 skiable acres (2,327 ha). At 11,666 feet (3,556 m), Lone Peak is the tallest summit of the resort's three mountains, giving Big Sky 4,350 feet (1,326 m) of vertical drop. There are 250 named runs, with the longest one stretching about 6 miles (9.6 km). The area gets about 400 inches (1,016 cm) of snowfall annually.

united states' largest ski resorts

total combined length of slopes in miles (km)

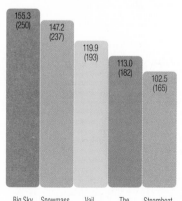

Big Sky Resort, Montana	Snowmass, Colorado	Vail, Colorado	The Canyons, Utah	Steamboat, Colorado
155.3 (250)	147.2 (237)	119.9 (193)	113.0 (182)	102.5 (165)

215

state with the world's largest indoor rain forest

Nebraska

At 123,000 square feet (11,427 sq m), the Lied Jungle at the Henry Doorly Zoo in Omaha is the world's largest indoor rain forest. The eight-story-tall building houses rain-forest exhibits from Asia, Africa, and South America that include plants, trees, caves, cliffs, bridges, and waterfalls. Some ninety different animal species live in these exhibits, including gibbons, small-clawed otters, spider monkeys, pygmy hippos, tapirs, and many birds and reptiles. Some exotic tree species include chocolate, allspice, African sausage, and black pepper. The giant roof lets in sunlight to promote natural growth. The jungle opened in 1992 and cost $15 million to create.

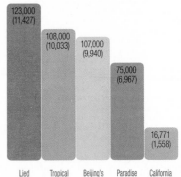

world's largest indoor rain forests

size in square feet (square meters)

Lied Jungle, Nebraska	Tropical Islands, Germany	Beijing's National Hotel, China	Paradise Earth, Arizona	California Academy of Sciences, California
123,000 (11,427)	108,000 (10,033)	107,000 (9,940)	75,000 (6,967)	16,771 (1,558)

world's tallest Ferris wheel

Nevada

The gigantic High Roller Ferris wheel towers 550 feet (167 m) above the Las Vegas, Nevada, landscape. Opened to the public in March 2014, the wheel is the largest in the world. It has 28 passenger cars that are shaped like spheres, and each one can hold 40 people. It takes about 30 minutes to make one rotation. About 6.6 million pounds (2,993,710 kg) of steel were used to create the wheel. The High Roller is a focal point in The Linq—a new development on the strip that will include restaurants, stores, and attractions.

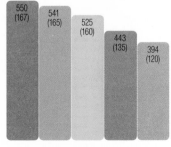

world's tallest Ferris wheels

height, in feet (m)

550 (167)	541 (165)	525 (160)	443 (135)	394 (120)
High Roller, Nevada	Singapore Flyer, Singapore	Star of Nanchang, China	London Eye, England	Suzhou Ferris Wheel, China

state with the oldest lottery

New Hampshire

New Hampshire was the first state to establish a legal lottery system when it sold its first ticket in 1964. The lottery was originally created to raise money for charitable causes throughout the state. Since it began, the New Hampshire Lottery has seen more than $4.1 billion in sales and other earnings—about $2.7 billion was paid out as prize money, and about $1.3 billion has gone to fund education in the state. The main in-state lottery in New Hampshire is called the Weekly Grand, but residents participate in several multistate lotteries as well.

states with the oldest lotteries

number of years in existence*

State	Years
New Hampshire	50
New York	47
New Jersey	44
Connecticut	43
Pennsylvania	43

*As of 2014

state with the world's longest boardwalk

New Jersey

The famous boardwalk in Atlantic City, New Jersey, stretches for 4 miles (6.4 km) along the beach. Combined with the adjoining boardwalk in Ventnor, the length increases to just under 6 miles (9.7 km). The 60-foot (18 m) wide boardwalk opened on June 26, 1870. It was the first boardwalk built in the United States, and was designed to keep sand out of the tourists' shoes. Today, the boardwalk is filled with amusement parks, shops, restaurants, and hotels. Some sections of the boardwalk were damaged during Superstorm Sandy in October 2012, but recovery efforts have restored much of the boardwalk to its original state.

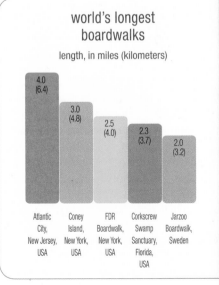

world's longest boardwalks

length, in miles (kilometers)

Atlantic City, New Jersey, USA	Coney Island, New York, USA	FDR Boardwalk, New York, USA	Corkscrew Swamp Sanctuary, Florida, USA	Jarzoo Boardwalk, Sweden
4.0 (6.4)	3.0 (4.8)	2.5 (4.0)	2.3 (3.7)	2.0 (3.2)

219

state with the highest state capital elevation

New Mexico

Santa Fe, New Mexico, sits 7,000 feet (2133.6 m) above sea level. That's 1.3 miles (2.1 km) high! It's located in the southern end of the Rocky Mountains, in the foothills of the Sangre de Cristo mountain range. Founded in 1610, it is one of the oldest capital cities in the United States. The city is home to about 70,000 residents, making it the fourth most-populated city in the state. Santa Fe is known for its diverse arts community, and draws many tourists each year to its museums and festivals.

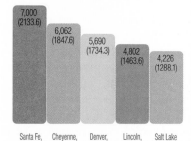

states with the highest state capital elevations

height above sea level, in feet (meters)

Santa Fe, New Mexico	Cheyenne, Wyoming	Denver, Colorado	Lincoln, Nebraska	Salt Lake City, Utah
7,000 (2133.6)	6,062 (1847.6)	5,690 (1734.3)	4,802 (1463.6)	4,226 (1288.1)

New York

New York City's Metropolitan Museum of Art draws about 6 million visitors each year. It is also the largest art museum in the US. The Met opened its doors on Fifth Avenue in March 1880, and has been expanding its building and growing its collections ever since. Today, the Met occupies a 2-million-square-foot (185,806 sq m) building, which contains about 2 million objects. Of these objects, tens of thousands are on display at any given time. Some of the popular areas of the museum include European Sculpture and Decorative Art, Greek and Roman Art, Egyptian Art, Asian Art, and the American Wing.

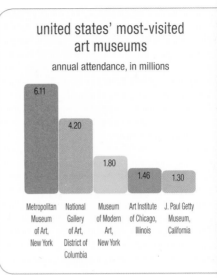

united states' most-visited art museums

annual attendance, in millions

Museum	Attendance
Metropolitan Museum of Art, New York	6.11
National Gallery of Art, District of Columbia	4.20
Museum of Modern Art, New York	1.80
Art Institute of Chicago, Illinois	1.46
J. Paul Getty Museum, California	1.30

state with the tallest lighthouse

North Carolina

The Cape Hatteras lighthouse in North Carolina rises 200 feet (60.9 m) above the Atlantic Ocean. The lighthouse protects ships from a dangerous stretch of the Atlantic coast that includes a 12-mile (19.3 km) sandbar known as Diamond Shoals. The lighthouse was first lit in October 1870, and was assigned the distinctive black-and-white stripe pattern. Cape Hatteras lighthouse is open to the public during spring and summer, and visitors can climb its 248 iron stairs to the top. That's the equivalent of climbing a 12-story building. The lighthouse is maintained by the National Park Service.

united states' tallest lighthouses

height in feet (meters)

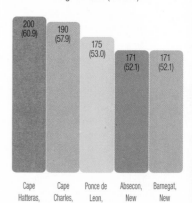

Cape Hatteras, North Carolina	Cape Charles, Virginia	Ponce de Leon, Florida	Absecon, New Jersey	Barnegat, New Jersey
200 (60.9)	190 (57.9)	175 (53.0)	171 (52.1)	171 (52.1)

state with the tallest scrap metal sculpture

North Dakota

In August 2001, Gary Greff created a 110-foot (33.5 m) tall metal sculpture along the stretch of road between Gladstone and Regent, North Dakota. That's the height of an 11-story building! The 154-foot (46.9 m) wide sculpture is called *Geese in Flight*, and shows Canada geese traveling across the prairie. Greff has created several other towering sculptures nearby, and the road has become known as the Enchanted Highway. He created these sculptures to attract tourists to the area and to support his hometown. He relies only on donations to finance his work.

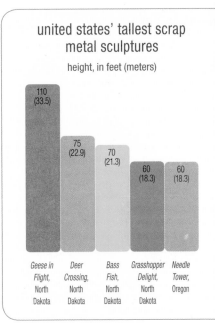

united states' tallest scrap metal sculptures

height, in feet (meters)

Sculpture	Height
Geese in Flight, North Dakota	110 (33.5)
Deer Crossing, North Dakota	75 (22.9)
Bass Fish, North Dakota	70 (21.3)
Grasshopper Delight, North Dakota	60 (18.3)
Needle Tower, Oregon	60 (18.3)

state with the largest individual indoor waterpark

Ohio

The Kalahari Resort and Convention Center in Sandusky, Ohio, is the largest indoor water park under one roof at 173,000 square feet (16072 sq m). Named after the African desert, the resort has a safari theme featuring African animals and trees. The resort features a 13,000-square-foot (1,208 sq-m) wave pool. In addition, two FlowRider areas use 50,000 gallons (220,224 l) of water to create 5-foot (1.5 m) waves for guests to try surfing and boogie boarding. Little guests can enjoy Crocodile Cove—a 3,000-square-foot (279 sq-m) activity pool. There's also a 920-foot (280 m) lazy river for guests who need to relax.

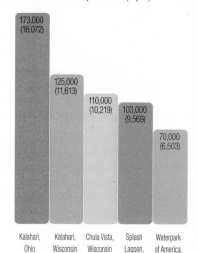

united states' largest individual indoor waterparks

area in square feet (sq m)

Kalahari, Ohio	Kalahari, Wisconsin	Chula Vista, Wisconsin	Splash Lagoon, Pennsylvania	Waterpark of America, Minnesota
173,000 (16,072)	125,000 (11,613)	110,000 (10,219)	103,000 (9,569)	70,000 (6,503)

state with the world's longest multiple-arch dam

Oklahoma

With a length of 6,565 feet (2,001 m), the Pensacola Dam in Oklahoma is the world's longest multiple-arch dam. Built in 1940, the dam is located on the Grand River and contains the Grand Lake o' the Cherokees—one of the largest reservoirs in the country, with 46,500 surface acres (18,818 ha) of water. The dam stands 145 feet (44 m) high. It was made out of 535,000 cubic yards of concrete, some 655,000 barrels of cement, another 10 million pounds (4.5 million kg) of structural steel, and 75,000 pounds (340,194 kg) of copper. The dam cost $27 million to complete.

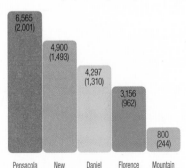

world's longest multiple-arch dams

length, in feet (meters)

Pensacola Dam, Oklahoma, USA	6,565 (2,001)
New Waddell Dam, Arizona, USA	4,900 (1,493)
Daniel Johnson Dam, Canada	4,297 (1,310)
Florence Lake Dam, California, USA	3,156 (962)
Mountain Dell Dam, Utah, USA	800 (244)

state with the deepest lake

Oregon

At a depth of 1,932 feet (589 m), Crater Lake in southern Oregon partially fills the remains of an old volcanic basin. The crater was formed almost 7,700 years ago when Mount Mazama erupted and then collapsed. The lake averages about 5 miles (8 km) in diameter. Crater Lake National Park—the nation's fifth-oldest park— surrounds the majestic lake and measures 249 square miles (645 sq km). The area's large snowfalls average 530 inches (1,346 cm) a year, and supply Crater Lake with its water. In addition to being the United States' deepest lake, it's also the eighth-deepest lake in the world.

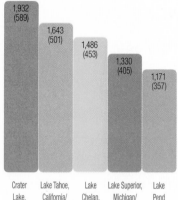

united states' deepest lakes

greatest depth, in feet (meters)

Crater Lake, Oregon	Lake Tahoe, California/ Nevada	Lake Chelan, Washington	Lake Superior, Michigan/ Minnesota/ Wisconsin	Lake Pend Oreille, Idaho
1,932 (589)	1,643 (501)	1,486 (453)	1,330 (405)	1,171 (357)

state with the oldest operating drive-in theater

Pennsylvania

Shankweiler's Drive-in Theatre opened in 1934. It was the country's second drive-in theater, and is the oldest one still operating today. Located in Orefield, Pennsylvania, the single-screen theater can accommodate 320 cars. Approximately 90 percent of the theater's guests are children. Although they originally used sound boxes located beside the cars, today's patrons can tune into a special radio station to hear the movies' music and dialogue. Shankweiler's is open from April to September.

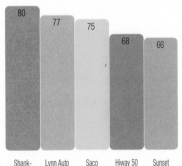

united states' oldest operating drive-in theaters

number of years open*

80	77	75	68	66
Shank-weiler's Drive-in Theatre, Pennsylvania (1934)	Lynn Auto Theatre, Ohio (1937)	Saco Drive-in, Maine (1939)	Hiway 50 Drive-in Theater, Tennessee (1946)	Sunset Drive-in Theatre, Pennsylvania (1948)

*As of 2014

227

state with the oldest temple
Rhode Island

The Touro Synagogue was dedicated during Hanukkah in December 1763 and is the oldest temple in the United States. Located in Newport, Rhode Island, the temple was designed by famous architect Peter Harrison and took four years to complete. In addition to serving as a symbol of religious freedom, the temple played another part in the country's history. When the British captured Newport in 1776, the temple briefly became a British hospital. Then, in 1781, George Washington met General Lafayette there to plan the final battles of the Revolution.

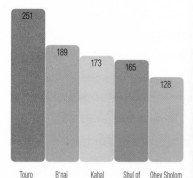

united states' oldest temples

number of years since dedication*

Touro Synagogue, Rhode Island (1763)	B'nai Jeshurun, New York (1825)	Kahal Kadosh Beth Elohim Synagogue, South Carolina (1841)	Shul of New York, New York (1849)	Ohev Sholom Talmud Torah, District of Columbia (1886)
251	189	173	165	128

*As of 2014

state with the oldest museum

South Carolina

The Charleston Museum in Charleston, South Carolina, was founded in 1773—three years before the Declaration of Independence was signed. The museum was founded to preserve the culture and history of the southern town and the surrounding area, and opened its doors to the public in 1824. Some of the exhibits in the museum include furniture, silver, and art made in the area, as well as fossils of local birds and animals. Two historic houses, which were built between 1772 and 1803, are also run by the museum. Visitors can tour these homes to learn about the state's early architecture.

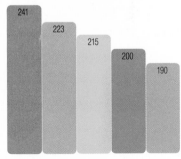

united states' oldest museums

number of years open*

Museum	Years
Charleston Museum, South Carolina (1773)	241
Albany Institute of History & Art, New York (1791)	223
Peabody Essex Museum, Massachusetts (1799)	215
Peale Museum, Maryland (1814)	200
Pilgrim Hall, Massachusetts (1824)	190

*As of 2014

229

state with the largest petrified wood collection

South Dakota

Lemmon's Petrified Wood Park in South Dakota is home to 30 acres (12.1 ha) of petrified wood. It covers an entire city block in downtown Lemmon. It was built between 1930 and 1932 when locals collected petrified wood from the area and constructed displays. One structure in the park—known as the Castle—weighs more than 300 tons (272 t) and is made partly from petrified wood and partly of petrified dinosaur and mammoth bones. Other exhibits include a wishing well, a waterfall, the Lemmon Pioneer Museum, and hundreds of pile sculptures.

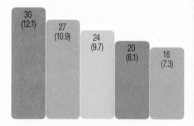

united states' largest petrified wood collections

area, in acres (hectares)

Lemmon's Petrified Wood Park, South Dakota	Long Logs Forest, Arizona	Rainbow Forest, Arizona	Crystal Forest, Arizona	Black Forest, Arizona
30 (12.1)	27 (10.9)	24 (9.7)	20 (8.1)	18 (7.3)

state with the world's largest freshwater aquarium

Tennessee

The Tennessee Aquarium in Chattanooga is an impressive 130,000 square feet (12,077 sq m), making it the largest freshwater aquarium in the world. The $45 million building holds a total of 400,000 gallons (1,514,165 L) of water. In addition, the aquarium features a 60,000-square-foot (5,574 sq m) building dedicated to the ocean and the creatures that live there. Permanent features in the aquarium include a discovery hall and an environmental learning lab. Some of the aquarium's 12,000 animals include alligators, paddlefish, lake sturgeon, sea dragons, and snapping turtles. And to feed all of these creatures, the aquarium goes through 12,000 crickets, 33,300 worms, and 1,200 pounds (545 kg) of seafood each month!

world's largest freshwater aquariums

size, in square feet (square meters)

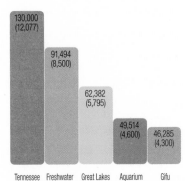

130,000 (12,077)	Tennessee Aquarium, Tennessee, USA
91,494 (8,500)	Freshwater Center, Denmark
62,382 (5,795)	Great Lakes Aquarium, Minnesota, USA
49,514 (4,600)	Aquarium of the Lakes, UK
46,285 (4,300)	Gifu Freshwater Aquarium, Japan

231

state with the most popular football team

Texas

The Houston Texans were cheered on by 704,345 fans at Reliant Stadium in 2013. However, the team—which was formed in 2002—didn't have its best season that year. They only won the first 2 of their 16 games and finished in last place in the AFC South division. The team was lead by head coach Gary Kubiak and quarterback Ryan Fitzpatrick. In 2014, Kubiak was replaced by Bill O'Brien. One fan favorite at the stadium was the installation of new high-definition video boards that are the largest in the world.

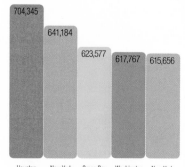

states with the most popular football teams

total attendance in 2013

Houston Texans, TX	New York Giants, NY	Green Bay Packers, WI	Washington Redskins, DC	New York Jets, NY
704,345	641,184	623,577	617,767	615,656

state with the largest dinosaur collection

Utah

The Museum of Ancient Life at the Thanksgiving Point Institute in Lehi, Utah, has the largest dinosaur collection in the country with 60 complete skeletons on display. Guests are even invited to touch some of the real fossils, bones, and eggs on exhibit. There are about 50 interactive displays throughout the Museum of Ancient Life. Guests touring the museum can also observe a working paleontology lab. The museum, which opened in June 2000, holds a sleepover once a month for kids to go on a behind-the-scenes tour.

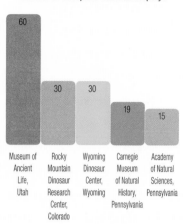

united states' largest dinosaur collections

number of complete skeletal displays

Museum of Ancient Life, Utah	Rocky Mountain Dinosaur Research Center, Colorado	Wyoming Dinosaur Center, Wyoming	Carnegie Museum of Natural History, Pennsylvania	Academy of Natural Sciences, Pennsylvania
60	30	30	19	15

state that produces the most maple syrup

Vermont

Maple syrup production in Vermont totaled more than 1.3 million gallons (4.996 L) in 2013 and accounted for about 40 percent of the United States' total yield that year. There are approximately 3.8 million tree taps used by the state's 2,000 maple syrup producers, and the annual production generates more than $20 million. It takes about five tree taps to collect enough maple sap—approximately 40 gallons (151.4 L)—to produce just 1 gallon (3.79 L) of syrup. Vermont maple syrup is also made into maple sugar, maple cream, and maple candies.

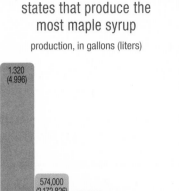

states that produce the most maple syrup

production, in gallons (liters)

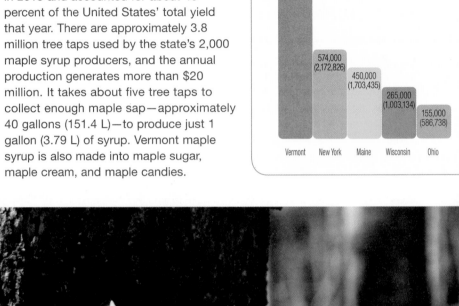

- Vermont: 1.320 (4.996)
- New York: 574,000 (2,172,826)
- Maine: 450,000 (1,703,435)
- Wisconsin: 265,000 (1,003,134)
- Ohio: 155,000 (586,738)

state with the oldest horse show

Virginia

The Upper Colt & Horse Show in Upperville, Virginia, was first held in 1853, and has run every year since then. The show lasts for seven days, and features all levels of competition from beginning riders to Olympic champions. About 20,000 spectators turn out each year to watch the more than 2,000 horse-and-rider combinations. In addition to the horse show, visitors can enjoy an arts & crafts fair, boutiques, food vendors, children's games, and a basset hound demonstration.

united states' oldest horse shows

years continuously held, as of 2014

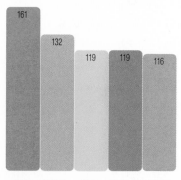

Upper Colt & Horse Show, Virginia	National Horse Show, Kentucky	Devon Horse Show, Pennsylvania	Monmouth Horse Show, New Jersey	Warrenton Horse Show, Virginia
161	132	119	119	116

state with the longest train tunnel

Washington

The Cascade Tunnel runs through the Cascade Mountains in central Washington and measures 7.8 miles (12.6 km) long. The tunnel connects the towns of Berne and Scenic. It was built by the Great Northern Railway in 1929 to replace the original tunnel, which was built at an elevation frequently hit with snowslides. To help cool the trains' diesel engines and remove fumes, the tunnel is equipped with huge fans that blow air while and after a train passes.

united states' longest train tunnels

length, in miles (kilometers)

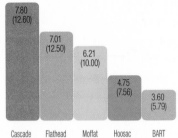

Tunnel	Length
Cascade Tunnel, Washington	7.80 (12.60)
Flathead Tunnel, Missouri	7.01 (12.50)
Moffat Tunnel, Colorado	6.21 (10.00)
Hoosac Tunnel, Massachusetts	4.75 (7.56)
BART Transbay Tube, California	3.60 (5.79)

CASCADE TUNNEL
7.8 MILES LONG   ELEVATION 2247 FEET
41,152 FEET LONG   COMPLETED 1928

state with the longest steel arch bridge

West Virginia

With a main span of 1,700 feet (518 m) and a weight of about 88 million pounds (40 million kg), the New River Gorge Bridge in Fayetteville, West Virginia, is the longest and largest steel arch bridge in the United States. It is approximately 875 feet (267 m) above the New River and is the second-highest bridge in the country. After three years of construction, the bridge was completed in 1977. The $37 million structure is the focus of Bridge Day—a statewide annual festival that is one of the largest extreme sports events in the United States, drawing hundreds of BASE jumpers and thousands of spectators.

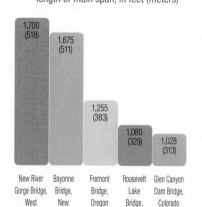

united states' longest steel arch bridges

length of main span, in feet (meters)

1,700 (518)	1,675 (511)	1,255 (383)	1,080 (329)	1,028 (313)
New River Gorge Bridge, West Virginia	Bayonne Bridge, New Jersey	Fremont Bridge, Oregon	Roosevelt Lake Bridge, Arizona	Glen Canyon Dam Bridge, Colorado

237

state with the oldest velodrome

Wisconsin

The Washington Park Velodrome in Kenosha, Wisconsin, was built in 1927 and is the oldest in the country. A velodrome, which is an arena used for cycling, has steeply banked oval tracks with two curves and two straightaways. The Washington Park Velodrome's 1,092-foot (333 m) track was originally made of clay but was later upgraded to asphalt. It's open to the public, but the Kenosha Velodrome Association also holds weekly races there during the summer. On non-race days, the track can be used for jogging and rollerblading. There are only about 40 velodromes in America.

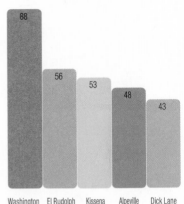

united states' oldest velodromes

years in continuous operation, as of 2015

Washington Park Velodrome, Wisconsin	El Rudolph Velodrome, Illinois	Kissena Velodrome, New York	Alpeville Velodrome, Oregon	Dick Lane Velodrome, Georgia
88	56	53	48	43

state that produces the most coal

Wyoming

Wyoming produced 388 million tons (351.9 million t) of coal in 2013—about 40 percent of the nation's total. Of the top-ten coal-producing mines in the United States, nine of them are in Wyoming. In fact, the top two mines—North Antelope Rochelle and Black Thunder—produce 20 percent of the country's coal. North Antelope Rochelle mine produced 108 million tons (97.9 million t), and Black Thunder contributed 93 million tons (84.3 million t). Wyoming's top ten mines are all located along the Powder River Basin. Wyoming has about a 42-billion-ton (38.1 billion t) reserve of recoverable coal.

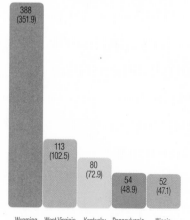

states that produce the most coal

coal production in 2013, in millions of tons (metric tons)

Wyoming	388 (351.9)
West Virginia	113 (102.5)
Kentucky	80 (72.9)
Pennsylvania	54 (48.9)
Illinois	52 (47.1)

Sports Records

olympics
basketball
football
golf
baseball
running
tennis
soccer
car racing
motorcycling
horse racing
hockey

Sensational Season

Peyton Manning and the Denver Broncos shattered records during the 2013 NFL season. The quarterback threw for 55 touchdown passes that year—five more than the previous record set by the New England Patriots in 2007. He also scored a total of 606 points, topping the 589 points scored by the Patriots in 2007. Finally, Manning completed 5,477 passing yards in 2013—one more than Drew Brees in 2011.

Sweet Shot

Harlem Globetrotter Corey "Thunder" Law scored the longest basketball shot ever when he sunk a basket from 109 feet and 9 inches (33.4 m) on November 14, 2013. That's actually longer than a regulation 94-foot (28.6 m) NBA court! Law stood in the stands at the Phoenix Suns' US Airways Arena when he made history.

Mega Match Minutes

Tennis pros John Isner (USA) and Nicolas Mahut (France) battled it out on the All England Club courts for 11 hours and 5 minutes on June 24, 2010. Isner eventually won the duel that ended in a 70-to-68 fifth set tiebreaker. It took place in the first round of the Wimbledon men's singles tournament.

PLAYER	SETS	GAMES	POI
Nicolas MAHUT			
John ISNER			

Slam-tastic

St. Louis Cardinal Fernando Tatis achieved the unthinkable on April 23, 1999—he hit two grand slams in the same inning. Although two home runs by the same player in the same inning has happened in MLB 57 times, two grand slams have not. The Cardinals went on to beat the Los Angeles Dodgers with a score of 11 to 5.

Grab a Broom

During the 2014 Sochi Olympic Games, there were eight podium sweeps— athletes from the same country won the gold, silver, and bronze medals in the same event. The Netherlands swept four speed skating events, the USA and France both swept men's freestyle skiing competitions, and Norway and Russia dominated in cross-country skiing races.

Not a Lot of Elbow Room

When the Detroit Red Wings met the Toronto Maple Leafs at the 2014 NHL Winter Classic, more than 100,000 fans crowded into Michigan Stadium—an NHL attendance record. The NHL sold 105,491 tickets to the January 1, 2014, outdoor regular season game, but weather conditions and late admission made it hard to get an exact count of how many showed up to cheer on the teams.

Cha-Ching

The highest transfer fee in professional soccer—$131.8 million—was earned by Cristiano Ronaldo when he moved from Manchester United to Real Madrid in July 2009. In October 2013, Gareth Bale came in a close second, earning $123 million when he transferred from Trottenham to Real Madrid.

country with the most Olympic speed skating medals

Netherlands

Athletes from the Netherlands have won 105 Olympic speed skating medals since the sport was first contested at the 1924 Olympic Games. The country's hardware includes 35 gold, 36 silver, and 34 bronze medals. The Netherlands had an especially strong showing at the 2014 Olympics in Sochi, Russia, where the male skaters won 5 of the 6 individual events, and the women won 3 of the 6 individual events. In fact, all of the nation's 24 medals in 2014 came from a speed track event. Three athletes also set Olympic speed records. Some of the Netherland's current skaters include Sven Kramer, Antoinette de Jong, Michel Mulder, and Ireen Wüst.

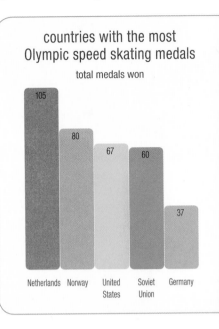

countries with the most Olympic speed skating medals

total medals won

105	80	67	60	37
Netherlands	Norway	United States	Soviet Union	Germany

Sven Kramer

Shaun White

country with the most Olympic snowboarding medals

United States

With a total of 24 Olympic medals, US athletes are tops in snowboarding. The nation's impressive collection includes 10 gold, 5 silver, and 9 bronze medals. The most successful US snowboarder is Kelly Clark, who won a total of 3 medals—more than any other snowboarder in the world. Shaun White and Seth Wescott are the only two US athletes who have won two gold medals. Snowboarding first appeared in the Olympics in 1998, and the US has been in each of the competitions since then. The country's most successful year was 2006 in Turin, Italy, when athletes brought home a total of 7 medals.

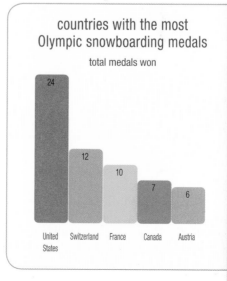

countries with the most Olympic snowboarding medals

total medals won

United States	24
Switzerland	12
France	10
Canada	7
Austria	6

Meryl Davis and Charlie White

country with the most Olympic figure skating medals

United States

The United States has dominated Olympic figure skating, picking up a total of 48 medals since the event was first featured in 1908. The medal collection includes 15 gold, 16 silver, and 17 bronze. The US has competed in 24 of the 26 Olympic skating competitions, and had its most successful year in 1956 when athletes picked up 5 medals. Men's and ladies' singles have been included in the Games since it began, while ice dancing was added in 1976. A new competition—mixed team—was added in 2014. Some of the US's recent medal winners include Meryl Davis and Charlie White, an ice-dancing team that won gold in Sochi in 2014.

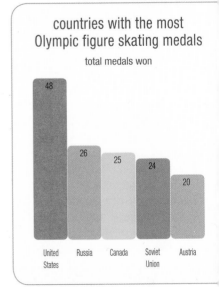

countries with the most Olympic figure skating medals

total medals won

United States	Russia	Canada	Soviet Union	Austria
48	26	25	24	20

country with the most winter Olympic medals

Norway

Norway is the most successful country in the winter Olympic Games with a total medal count of 329—118 gold, 111 silver, and 100 bronze. Norway has competed in every winter Games since it was first held in 1924, and it has led the medal count in 7 of them. Norway won the most medals as the home team in Lillehammer in 1994, and in Sochi, Russia, in 2014, where the picked up 26 medals at each Games. Norwegians have had the most success in cross-country skiing (107 medals), speed skating (80 medals), and biathlon (35 medals). Some of Norway's recent gold-medal winners at the 2014 Sochi Games include Marit Bjoergen (cross country), Ole Einar Bjoerndalen (biathlon), and Joergen Graabak (Nordic combined).

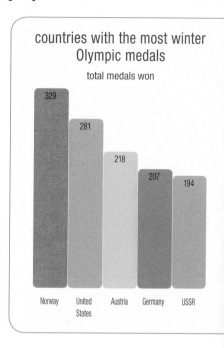

countries with the most winter Olympic medals

total medals won

Country	Medals
Norway	329
United States	281
Austria	218
Germany	207
USSR	194

Marit Bjoergen

nba team with the most championship titles

Boston Celtics

The Boston Celtics are the most successful team in the NBA with 17 championship wins. The first win came in 1957, and the team went on to win the next seven consecutive titles—the longest streak of consecutive championship wins in the history of US sports. The most recent championship title came in 2008. The Celtics entered the Basketball Association of America in 1946, which later merged into the NBA in 1949. The Celtics made the NBA play-offs for four consecutive seasons from 2001 to 2005, but they were eliminated in early rounds each time.

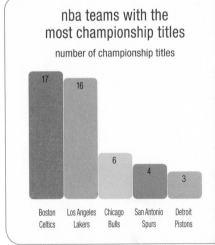

nba teams with the most championship titles

number of championship titles

Boston Celtics	Los Angeles Lakers	Chicago Bulls	San Antonio Spurs	Detroit Pistons
17	16	6	4	3

nba player with the highest career scoring average

Wilt Chamberlain & Michael Jordan

Both Michael Jordan and Wilt Chamberlain averaged an amazing 30.1 points per game during their legendary careers. Jordan played for the Chicago Bulls and the Washington Wizards. He led the league in scoring for seven years. During the 1986 season, he became the second person ever to score 3,000 points in a single season. Chamberlain played for the Philadelphia Warriors, the Philadelphia 76ers, and the Los Angeles Lakers. In addition to the highest scoring average, he holds the record for the most games scoring 50 points or more, with 118.

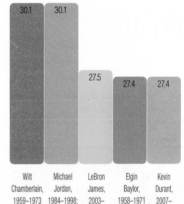

nba players with the highest career scoring averages

average points per game

30.1	30.1	27.5	27.4	27.4
Wilt Chamberlain, 1959–1973	Michael Jordan, 1984–1998; 2001–2003	LeBron James, 2003–	Elgin Baylor, 1958–1971	Kevin Durant, 2007–

Michael Jordan

BULLS 23

nba's highest-scoring game

Detroit Pistons

On December 13, 1983, the Detroit Pistons beat the Denver Nuggets with a score of 186–184 at McNichols Arena in Denver, Colorado. The game was tied at 145 at the end of regular play, and three overtime periods were needed to determine the winner. During the game, both the Pistons and the Nuggets each had six players who scored in the double digits. Four players scored more than 40 points each, which was an NBA first. The Pistons scored 74 field goals that night, claiming another NBA record that still stands today.

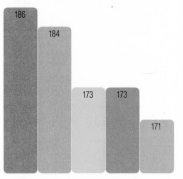

nba's highest-scoring games
points scored by a team in one game

186	184	173	173	171
Detroit Pistons, vs. Denver Nuggets, 1983	Denver Nuggets, vs. Detroit Pistons, 1983	Boston Celtics, vs. Minneapolis Lakers, 1959	Phoenix Suns, vs. Denver Nuggets, 1990	San Antonio Spurs, vs. Milwaukee Bucks, 1982

nba player with the highest salary

Kobe Bryant

Kobe Bryant earns $30.5 million a year playing as a guard for the LA Lakers. Bryant has been a Laker since he turned pro in 1996. During his 18 years in the NBA, he has scored more than 31,700 points and grabbed more than 6,601 rebounds. Bryant has also logged almost 45,567 minutes on the court. He was a five-time NBA Champion between 2000 and 2010, and he was the NBA Most Valuable Player during the 2007–2008 season. He has also earned All-NBA honors every year since 2002. In 2008 and 2012, Bryant helped Team USA win the gold medal at the Beijing and London Olympics.

nba players with the highest salaries

annual salary, in millions of US dollars

Kobe Bryant	Dirk Nowitzki	Amar'e Stoudemire	Carmelo Anthony	Dwight Howard
30.5	22.7	21.7	21.4	20.5

nba player with the highest field goal percentage

Artis Gilmore

Artis Gilmore leads the NBA with the highest career field goal percentage at .599. He was drafted by the Chicago Bulls in 1971, and went on to also play for the San Antonio Spurs and the Boston Celtics before retiring in 1988. A center who towered more than 7 feet (2 m) tall, Gilmore had 9,161 rebounds and 1,747 blocks. He also scored 15,579 points and had 1,777 assists. He was a five-time NBA All Star between 1978 and 1986. Gilmore, who was nicknamed the A-Train, played 909 regular season games.

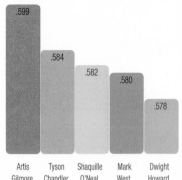

nba players with the highest field goal percentages

career field goal percentages

Artis Gilmore, 1971–1988	Tyson Chandler, 2001–	Shaquille O'Neal, 1992–2011	Mark West, 1983–2000	Dwight Howard, 2004–
.599	.584	.582	.580	.578

nba player with the most career points
Kareem Abdul-Jabbar

During his highly successful career, Kareem Abdul-Jabbar scored a total of 38,387 points. In 1969, Abdul-Jabbar began his NBA tenure with the Milwaukee Bucks. He was named Rookie of the Year in 1970. The following year he scored 2,596 points and helped the Bucks win the NBA championship. He was traded to the Los Angeles Lakers in 1975, and with his new team, Abdul-Jabbar won the NBA championship in 1980, 1982, 1985, 1987, and 1988. He retired from basketball in 1989 and was inducted into the Basketball Hall of Fame in 1995.

nba players with the most career points

points scored

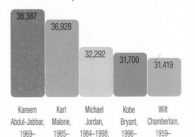

Kareem Abdul-Jabbar, 1969–1989	Karl Malone, 1985–2004	Michael Jordan, 1984–1998; 2001–2003	Kobe Bryant, 1996–	Wilt Chamberlain, 1959–1973
38,387	36,928	32,292	31,700	31,419

253

wnba player with the highest career ppg average

Cynthia Cooper

Cynthia Cooper has the highest scoring average in the WNBA with 21 points per game. During the play-offs, she has averaged 23.3 points per game. Cooper joined the league in 1997 as a Houston Comet and remained there for four years. After a two-year hiatus, she returned for a year, and then retired in 2003. During her five years in the WNBA, she scored a total of 2,601 points. Cooper has a career high of 44 points in one game versus Sacramento in 1997. She won a gold medal in the 1988 Olympics in Seoul, the 1987 Pan American Games, and the 1990 FIBA World Championship.

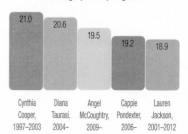

wnba players with the highest career ppg average

average points per game

21.0	20.6	19.5	19.2	18.9
Cynthia Cooper, 1997–2003	Diana Taurasi, 2004–	Angel McCoughtry, 2009–	Cappie Pondexter, 2006–	Lauren Jackson, 2001–2012

wnba player with the highest free-throw percentage

Elena Delle Donne

Chicago Sky forward/guard Elena Delle Donne has good aim—her free throw percentage is an awesome .929! Donne, who turned pro in 2013, is a graduate of the University of Delaware. She scored 543 points and grabbed 167 rebounds during her first year in the league. She was named 2013 Rookie of the Year. During her debut game, she scored 22 points—the third highest in WNBA history. She has also scored at least 20 points in 13 games during the 2013 season, which ranks her fifth in the league among rookie players.

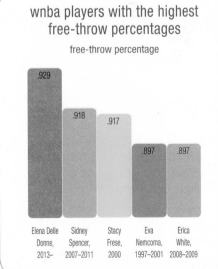

wnba players with the highest free-throw percentages

free-throw percentage

Player	Percentage
Elena Delle Donne, 2013–	.929
Sidney Spencer, 2007–2011	.918
Stacy Frese, 2000	.917
Eva Nemcoma, 1997–2001	.897
Erica White, 2008–2009	.897

wnba player with the most career points
Tina Thompson

A nine-time WNBA All-Star, Tina Thompson has scored 7,488 points during her 17-year career. The Los Angeles Sparks forward began her WNBA career in 1997 with the Houston Comets. She was the first draft pick in WNBA history. During her first four years with the Comets, she helped the team win the WNBA Championship each season and was the 2000 All-Star MVP. She joined the Los Angeles Sparks in 2009, and has a points-per-game average of 15.1. At the 2004 and 2008 Olympic Games, Thompson picked up gold medals for her role in helping Team USA dominate the competition.

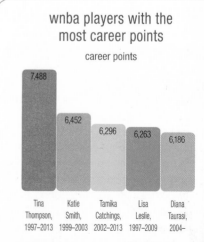

wnba players with the most career points
career points

Tina Thompson, 1997–2013	Katie Smith, 1999–2003	Tamika Catchings, 2002–2013	Lisa Leslie, 1997–2009	Diana Taurasi, 2004–
7,488	6,452	6,296	6,263	6,186

wnba player with the most career rebounds

Lisa Leslie

Lisa Leslie grabbed 3,307 rebounds during her 12-year career in the WNBA. Leslie joined the league during its inaugural season in 1997 when she was signed by the Los Angeles Sparks and remained with the team throughout her career. A three-time WNBA MVP and eight-time WNBA All Star, Leslie became the first woman to dunk in the league in 2002. In 2009, she again made history by becoming the first woman to score 6,000 points. Leslie won four Olympic gold medals between 1996 and 2008.

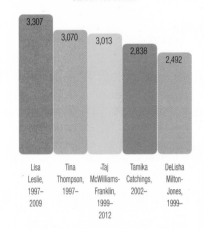

wnba players with the most career rebounds

career rebounds

Lisa Leslie, 1997–2009	Tina Thompson, 1997–	Taj McWilliams-Franklin, 1999–2012	Tamika Catchings, 2002–	DeLisha Milton-Jones, 1999–
3,307	3,070	3,013	2,838	2,492

257

women's basketball team with the most ncaa championships

UCONN

The UCONN Huskies have won the NCAA basketball championship 9 times. All 9 championships were celebrated between 1995 and 2014 under the leadership of Geno Auriemma. The team has qualified for the Final Four 15 times, and has won the Big East Tournament Championship 18 times. The Huskies have sent 23 players to the WNBA. Connecticut also holds the record for the most consecutive games won in the NCAA with 90 between April 2005 and December 2010. In 2013-2014, the Huskies had a perfect season, winning all 40 games.

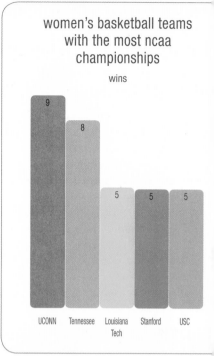

women's basketball teams with the most ncaa championships

wins

UCONN	Tennessee	Louisiana Tech	Stanford	USC
9	8	5	5	5

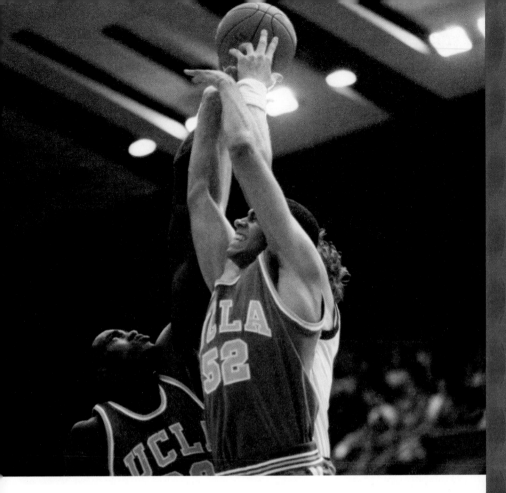

men's basketball team with the most ncaa championships

UCLA

With 11 titles, the University of California, Los Angeles (UCLA) has the most NCAA basketball championship wins. The Bruins won their 11th championship in 1995. The school has won 23 of their last 41 league titles and has been in the NCAA play-offs for 35 of the last 41 years. During the final round of the NCAA championship in 2006, UCLA lost to the Florida Gators with a score of 73–57. Not surprisingly, UCLA has produced some basketball legends, including Kareem Abdul-Jabbar, Reggie Miller, and Baron Davis. For the last 36 years, the Bruins have called Pauley Pavilion home.

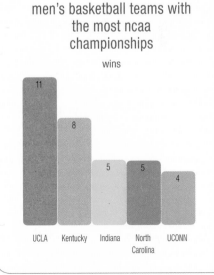

men's basketball teams with the most ncaa championships

wins

UCLA	Kentucky	Indiana	North Carolina	UCONN
11	8	5	5	4

259

nfl player with the most passing yards

Brett Favre

Quarterback Brett Favre knows how to hit his receivers: He completed 71,838 passing yards during his amazing career. He has a completion rate of 62 percent, and has connected for 508 touchdowns. Favre is also the NFL's all-time leader in passing touchdowns (508), completions (6,300), and attempts (10,169). Favre began his career with the Atlanta Falcons in 1991. He was traded to the Green Bay Packers the next season, and played for them until 2007. Favre joined the New York Jets for the season, and was then signed by the Minnesota Vikings for the 2009 season.

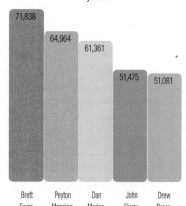

nfl players with the most passing yards

yards

Brett Favre, 1991–2010	Peyton Manning, 1998–	Dan Marino, 1983–2000	John Elway, 1983–1999	Drew Brees, 2001–
71,838	64,964	61,361	51,475	51,081

nfl player with the most career touchdowns

Jerry Rice

Jerry Rice has scored a record 208 touchdowns. He is widely considered to be one of the greatest wide receivers to ever play in the National Football League. Rice holds a total of 14 NFL records, including career receptions (1,549), receiving yards (22,895), receiving touchdowns (197), most games with 100 receiving yards (75), and many others. He was named NFL Player of the Year twice, *Sports Illustrated* Player of the Year four times, and NFL Offensive Player of the Year once. Rice retired from the NFL in 2005.

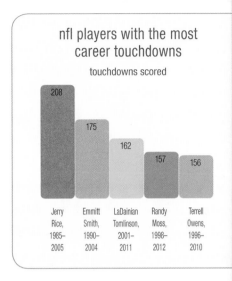

nfl players with the most career touchdowns

touchdowns scored

Jerry Rice, 1985–2005	Emmitt Smith, 1990–2004	LaDainian Tomlinson, 2001–2011	Randy Moss, 1998–2012	Terrell Owens, 1996–2010
208	175	162	157	156

nfl player with the most single-season touchdowns

LaDainian Tomlinson

Running back LaDainian Tomlinson scored 31 touchdowns during the 2006 season. He was also named NFL Most Valuable Player that season for his outstanding performance. During his pro career, he scored a total of 138 touchdowns. Tomlinson was selected fifth overall in the 2001 draft by the San Diego Chargers but was traded to the New York Jets in 2010. He holds several Chargers records, including 372 rushing attempts (2002), 100 receptions (2003), and 1,815 rushing yards in a season (2006). Tomlinson was named to five Pro Bowls and retired in 2012.

nfl players with the most single-season touchdowns
touchdowns scored

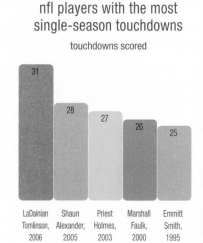

LaDainian Tomlinson, 2006	Shaun Alexander, 2005	Priest Holmes, 2003	Marshall Faulk, 2000	Emmitt Smith, 1995
31	28	27	26	25

nfl player with the highest career scoring total

Morten Andersen

Morten Andersen led the NFL in scoring with a career total of 2,544 points. He made 565 field goals out of 709 attempts, giving him a 79.7 percent completion rate. He scored 849 extra points out of 859 attempts, resulting in a 98.8 percent success rate. Andersen, a placekicker who began his career in 1982 with the New Orleans Saints, retired in 2008 after playing for the Atlanta Falcons. Known as the Great Dane, partly because of his birthplace of Denmark, Andersen played 382 professional games. His most successful season was in 1995, when he scored 122 points.

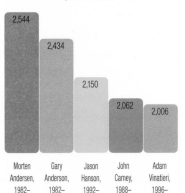

nfl players with the highest career scoring totals

points scored

Morten Andersen, 1982–2008	Gary Anderson, 1982–2005	Jason Hanson, 1992–2012	John Carney, 1988–2010	Adam Vinatieri, 1996–
2,544	2,434	2,150	2,062	2,006

nfl coach with the most wins
Don Shula

Don Shula led his teams to a remarkable 347 wins during his 33 years as a head coach in the National Football League. When Shula became head coach of the Baltimore Colts in 1963, he became the youngest head coach in football history. He stayed with the team until 1969 and reached the play-offs four times. Shula became the head coach for the Miami Dolphins in 1970 and coached them until 1995. During this time, the Dolphins reached the play-offs 20 times and won at least 10 games a season 21 times. After leading them to Super Bowl wins in 1972 and 1973, Shula became one of only five coaches to win the championship in back-to-back years.

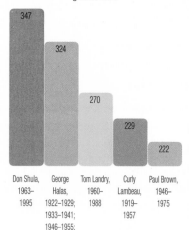

nfl coaches with the most wins
games won

Coach	Games won
Don Shula, 1963–1995	347
George Halas, 1922–1929; 1933–1941; 1946–1955; 1958–1967	324
Tom Landry, 1960–1988	270
Curly Lambeau, 1919–1957	229
Paul Brown, 1946–1975	222

nfl player with the highest salary

Drew Brees

Quarterback Drew Brees earned a whopping $51 million during 2013. His salary with the New Orleans Saints accounts for $40 million of that total, and the other $11 comes from multiple endorsements. Some of the companies he pitches products for include Nike, Pepsi, Procter & Gamble, Verizon Wireless, and Wrangler. Brees was the second overall draft pick in 2001 by the San Diego Chargers, and he joined the Saints as a free agent in 2006. Brees was named Offensive Player of the Year in 2008 and MVP of Super Bowl XLIV in 2011. In 2010, he was named the *Sports Illustrated* Sportsman of the Year.

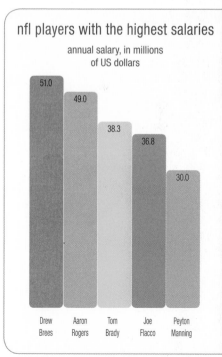

nfl players with the highest salaries
annual salary, in millions of US dollars

Drew Brees	Aaron Rogers	Tom Brady	Joe Flacco	Peyton Manning
51.0	49.0	38.3	36.8	30.0

265

nfl quarterback with the highest seasonal rating

Josh McCown

Josh McCown was the top quarterback in 2013 with a rating of 85.1. He was also named NFL Offensive Player of the Week during November of that year. Drafted by the Arizona Cardinals in 2002, McCown has also played for the Detroit Lions, the Oakland Raiders, the Miami Dolphins, the Carolina Panthers, the San Francisco 49ers, and the Chicago Bears. He most recently signed a two-year, $10 million contract with the Tampa Bay Buccaneers in 2014. During the last 11 seasons, McCown has thrown 54 touchdowns and 8,827 passing yards.

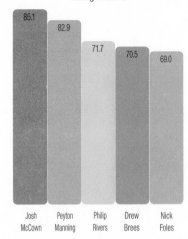

nfl quarterbacks with the highest seasonal rating

rating in 2013

Josh McCown	Peyton Manning	Philip Rivers	Drew Brees	Nick Foles
85.1	82.9	71.7	70.5	69.0

nfl team with the most super bowl wins

Pittsburgh Steelers

With six championship wins between 1974 and 2009, the Pittsburgh Steelers have won more Super Bowls than any other team in NFL history. The Steelers have also played and won more AFC championship games than any other team in the conference. The Steelers were founded in 1933 and are the fifth-oldest franchise in the league. Twenty-three retired Steelers have been inducted into the Pro Football Hall of Fame, including Franco Harris, Chuck Noll, and Terry Bradshaw.

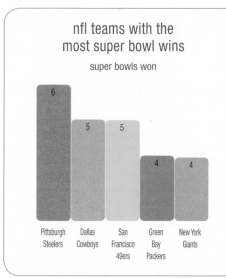

nfl teams with the most super bowl wins

super bowls won

Pittsburgh Steelers	Dallas Cowboys	San Francisco 49ers	Green Bay Packers	New York Giants
6	5	5	4	4

most valuable sporting event prize

UEFA Champions League

The UEFA Champions League—also known as the European Cup—awards the winning soccer team $65 million in prize money. The annual competition began in 1955 for the winning soccer team of each European country, but today countries can send up to four teams to compete. The main tournament includes 32 teams that are divided into eight groups. The winner of the UEFA Champions League qualifies for the FIFA Club World Cup. Real Madrid holds the record for most victories with ten wins. Twenty-two teams have won the big game, and twelve have won it more than once. The final game is extremely popular in Europe, drawing a television audience of about 170 million.

most valuable sporting events prizes

prize money paid to the winning team, in millions of US dollars

UEFA Champions League	65
FIFA World Cup	31
UEFA European Football Championship	29
World Series	19
UEFA Europa League	12

pga golfer with the lowest seasonal average

Steve Stricker

Steve Stricker led the PGA in 2013 with the lowest seasonal average of 68.94. During the season, he played 13 events and achieved four second-place finishes and 8 top-ten finishes. Stricker also earned $4.4 million in prize money. Since turning pro in 1990, he has won 21 professional tournaments, including 12 on the PGA tour. He was ranked among the top-ten golfers in the world for 57 consecutive weeks between 2007 and 2008, and then for another 157 weeks between 2009 and 2012.

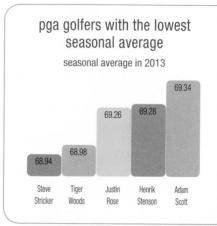

pga golfers with the lowest seasonal average

seasonal average in 2013

Steve Stricker	Tiger Woods	Justin Rose	Henrik Stenson	Adam Scott
68.94	68.98	69.26	69.28	69.34

lpga golfer with the lowest seasonal average

Stacy Lewis

American golfer Stacy Lewis had a seasonal average of 69.48, which was the lowest in the LPGA during 2013. During the year, she played 26 events, and had 19 top-ten finishes. Lewis also led the LPGA in birdies and eagles. She turned pro in 2008, and joined the LPGA the following year. Since then, she's won two major championships—the 2011 Kraft Nabisco Championship and the 2013 British Open. She was named the LPGA Player of the Year in 2012. Lewis's career earnings total more than $6.5 million.

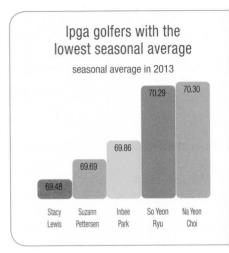

lpga golfers with the lowest seasonal average

seasonal average in 2013

Stacy Lewis	Suzann Pettersen	Inbee Park	So Yeon Ryu	Na Yeon Choi
69.48	69.69	69.86	70.29	70.30

lpga's highest-paid golfer
Annika Sorenstam

Annika Sorenstam has earned $22.5 million since her LPGA career began in 1994. During this time, she has had 72 career victories, including ten majors. In 2005, Sorenstam earned her eighth Rolex Player of the Year award—the most in LPGA history. She also became the first player to sweep Rolex Player of the Year honors, the Vare Trophy, and the ADT Official Money List title five times. Sorenstam earned her fifth consecutive Mizuno Classic title, making her the first golfer in LPGA history to win the same event five consecutive years. Sorenstam retired at the end of the 2008 season.

lpga's highest-paid golfers
career earnings, in millions of US dollars

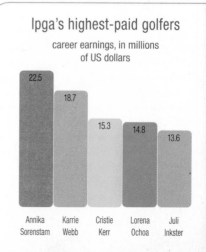

Annika Sorenstam	Karrie Webb	Cristie Kerr	Lorena Ochoa	Juli Inkster
22.5	18.7	15.3	14.8	13.6

golfer with the most major tournament wins

Jack Nicklaus

Golfing great Jack Nicklaus has won a total of 18 major championships. His wins include six Masters, five PGAs, four US Opens, and three British Opens. Nicklaus was named PGA Player of the Year five times. He was a member of the winning US Ryder Cup team six times and was an individual World Cup winner a record three times. He was inducted into the World Golf Hall of Fame in 1974, just 12 years after he turned professional. He joined the US Senior PGA Tour in 1990. In addition to playing the game, Nicklaus has designed close to 200 golf courses and has written a number of popular books about the sport.

golfers with the most major tournament wins

major tournament wins

Jack Nicklaus, 1962–1986	Tiger Woods, 1997–	Walter Hagen, 1914–1929	Ben Hogan, 1946–1953	Gary Player, 1959–1978
18	14	11	9	9

mlb player with the highest seasonal home-run total

Barry Bonds

On October 5, 2001, Barry Bonds smashed Mark McGwire's record for seasonal home runs when he hit his 71st home run in the first inning of a game against the Los Angeles Dodgers. In the third inning, he hit number 72, and two days later he reached 73. Bonds, a left fielder for the San Francisco Giants, has a career total of 762 home runs. He also holds the records for seasonal walks (232) and seasonal on-base percentage (.609). Bonds and his father, hitting coach Bobby Bonds, hold the all-time father-son home-run record with 1,020.

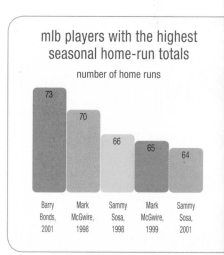

mlb players with the highest seasonal home-run totals

number of home runs

Barry Bonds, 2001	Mark McGwire, 1998	Sammy Sosa, 1998	Mark McGwire, 1999	Sammy Sosa, 2001
73	70	66	65	64

mlb team with the highest payroll

Los Angeles Dodgers

During the 2014 season, the Los Angeles Dodgers dished out more than $235.2 million for its payroll. That's a 6.3 percent increase from the previous season. The largest salaries went to pitcher Zack Greinke with $26 million, first baseman Adrian Gonzales with $21.8 million, and center-fielder Matt Kemp with $21.2 million. In all, 10 Dodgers earned $10 million or more during the season. About 51 percent of the payroll went to hitters, almost 42 percent went to pitchers, and nearly 7 percent went to people who didn't play.

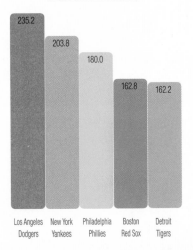

mlb teams with the highest payrolls

payroll in 2014,
in millions of US dollars

Los Angeles Dodgers	New York Yankees	Philadelphia Phillies	Boston Red Sox	Detroit Tigers
235.2	203.8	180.0	162.8	162.2

Matt Kemp

mlb player with the most home runs

Barry Bonds

Barry Bonds has hit more home runs than anyone who ever played in the MLB, cracking 762 balls over the wall during his ongoing career. Bonds has hit more than 30 home runs in a season 14 times—another MLB record. During his impressive career, Bonds has won 8 Gold Gloves, 12 Silver Slugger awards, and 14 All-Star games. Bonds began his career with the Pittsburgh Pirates in 1986; he was transferred to the San Francisco Giants in 1993 and played for the team until he retired. He is only one of three players to join the 700 Home Run Club.

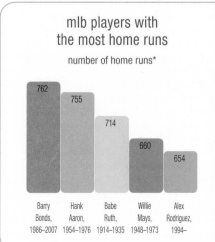

mlb players with the most home runs
number of home runs*

Player	Home runs
Barry Bonds, 1986–2007	762
Hank Aaron, 1954–1976	755
Babe Ruth, 1914–1935	714
Willie Mays, 1948–1973	660
Alex Rodriguez, 1994–	654

mlb pitcher with the most career strikeouts

Nolan Ryan

Nolan Ryan leads Major League Baseball with an incredible 5,714 career strikeouts. In his impressive 27-season career, he played for the New York Mets, the California Angels, the Houston Astros, and the Texas Rangers. The right-handed pitcher from Refugio, Texas, led the American League in strikeouts ten times. In 1989, at the age of 42, Ryan became the oldest pitcher ever to lead the Major Leagues in strikeouts. Ryan set another record in 1991 when he pitched his seventh career no-hitter.

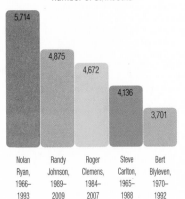

mlb pitchers with the most career strikeouts

number of strikeouts

Pitcher	Strikeouts
Nolan Ryan, 1966–1993	5,714
Randy Johnson, 1989–2009	4,875
Roger Clemens, 1984–2007	4,672
Steve Carlton, 1965–1988	4,136
Bert Blyleven, 1970–1992	3,701

mlb player with the most career hits

Pete Rose

Pete Rose belted an amazing 4,256 hits during his 23 years of professional baseball. He made his record-setting hit in 1985, when he was a player-manager for the Cincinnati Reds. By the time Rose retired as a player from Major League Baseball in 1986, he had set several other career records. Rose holds the Major League records for the most career games (3,562), the most times at bat (14,053), and the most seasons with more than 200 hits (10). During his career, he played for the Cincinnati Reds, the Philadelphia Phillies, and the Montreal Expos.

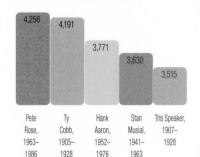

mlb players with the most career hits

number of hits

Player	Hits
Pete Rose, 1963–1986	4,256
Ty Cobb, 1905–1928	4,191
Hank Aaron, 1952–1976	3,771
Stan Musial, 1941–1963	3,630
Tris Speaker, 1907–1928	3,515

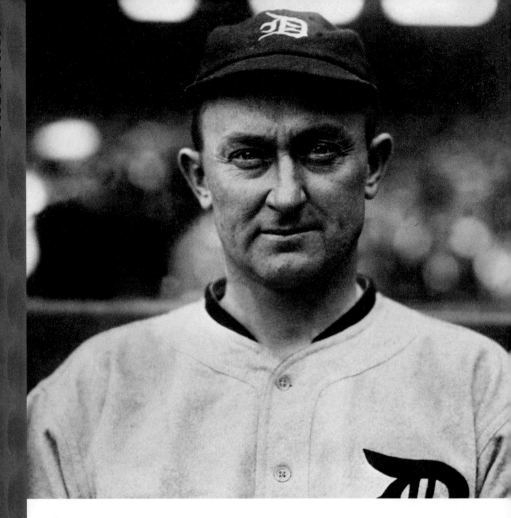

mlb player with the highest batting average

Ty Cobb

Baseball legend Ty Cobb had a batting average of .367 during his 23-year career, and it has remained the highest average in MLB history for more than 80 years. Known as the "Georgia Peach," the American League outfielder set 90 different MLB records during his outstanding career. He won 12 batting titles, including 9 consecutive wins between 1907 and 1915. Cobb began his career with the Detroit Tigers in 1905, and later moved to the Philadelphia Athletics in 1927. Cobb was voted into the Baseball Hall of Fame in 1936 with 98.2 percent of the votes.

mlb players with the highest batting average

highest career scoring average

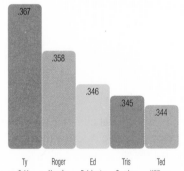

Ty Cobb, 1905–1928	Roger Hornsby, 1915–1937	Ed Delahanty, 1888–1903	Tris Speaker, 1907–1928	Ted Williams, 1939–1960
.367	.358	.346	.345	.344

mlb player with the most career runs
Rickey Henderson

During his 25 years in the majors, baseball great Rickey Henderson boasts the most career runs with 2,295. Henderson got his start with the Oakland Athletics in 1979, and went on to play for the Yankees, the Mets, the Mariners, the Red Sox, the Padres, the Dodgers, and the Angels. Henderson won a Gold Glove award in 1981, and the American League MVP award in 1989 and 1990. Henderson is also known as the "Man of Steal" because he holds the MLB record for most stolen bases in a career, with 1,406.

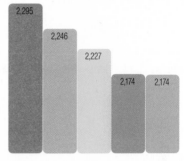

mlb players with the most career runs

number of career runs

Rickey Henderson, 1979–2003	Ty Cobb, 1905–1928	Barry Bonds, 1986–2007	Hank Aaron, 1954–1976	Babe Ruth, 1914–1935
2,295	2,246	2,227	2,174	2,174

279

Yogi Berra

most mvp awards in the american league

Yogi Berra, Joe DiMaggio, Jimmie Foxx, Mickey Mantle & Alex Rodriguez

With three honors each, Yogi Berra, Joe DiMaggio, Jimmie Foxx, Mickey Mantle, and Alex Rodriguez all hold the record for the most Most Valuable Player awards during their professional careers. Berra, DiMaggio, Mantle, and Rodriguez were all New York Yankees. Foxx played for the Athletics, the Cubs, and the Phillies. The player with the biggest gap between wins was DiMaggio, who won his first award in 1939 and his last in 1947. Also nicknamed "Joltin' Joe" and the "Yankee Clipper," DiMaggio began playing in the Major Leagues in 1936. The following year, he led the league in home runs and runs scored. He was inducted into the Baseball Hall of Fame in 1955.

mlb players with the most american league mvp awards

number of mvp awards

Yogi Berra, 1946–1963; 1965	Joe DiMaggio, 1936–1951	Jimmie Foxx, 1925–1945	Mickey Mantle, 1951–1968	Alex Rodriguez, 1994–
3	3	3	3	3

most mvp awards in the national league

Barry Bonds

San Francisco Giant Barry Bonds has earned seven Most Valuable Player awards for his amazing achievements in the National League. He received his first two MVP awards in 1990 and 1992 while playing for the Pittsburgh Pirates. The next five awards came while wearing the Giants uniform in 1993, 2001, 2002, 2003, and 2004. Bonds is the first player to win an MVP award three times in consecutive seasons. In fact, Bonds is the only baseball player in history to have won more than three MVP awards.

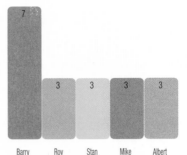

mlb players with the most national league mvp awards

number of mvp awards

Barry Bonds, 1986–2007	Roy Campanella, 1948–1957	Stan Musial, 1941–1963	Mike Schmidt, 1972–1989	Albert Pujols, 2001–
7	3	3	3	3

mlb team with the most world series wins

New York Yankees

Between 1923 and 2010, the New York Yankees were the World Series champions a record 27 times. The team picked up their latest win in October of 2009 when they beat the Philadelphia Phillies. The Yankees beat the Phillies 4 games to 2 to get their first win in nine years. Since their early days, the team has included some of baseball's greatest players, including Babe Ruth, Lou Gehrig, Yogi Berra, Joe DiMaggio, and Mickey Mantle.

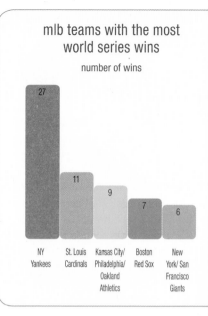

mlb teams with the most world series wins
number of wins

NY Yankees	St. Louis Cardinals	Kansas City/ Philadelphia/ Oakland Athletics	Boston Red Sox	New York/ San Francisco Giants
27	11	9	7	6

mlb pitcher with the most cy young awards

Roger Clemens

Roger Clemens, a starting pitcher for the Houston Astros, earned a record seven Cy Young Awards during his career. He set a Major League record in April 1986, when he struck out 20 batters in one game. He later tied this record in September 1996. In September 2001, Clemens became the first Major League pitcher to win 20 of his first 21 decisions in one season. In June 2003, he became the first pitcher in more than a decade to win his 300th game. He also struck out his 4,000th batter that year.

mlb pitchers with the most cy young awards

number of cy young awards

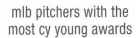

Roger Clemens, 1984–2007	Randy Johnson, 1988–2010	Steve Carlton, 1965–1988	Greg Maddux, 1986–2008	Pedro Martinez, 1992–2011
7	5	4	4	3

283

mlb player with the most at bats

Pete Rose

Pete Rose has stood behind the plate for 14,053 at bats—more than any other Major League player. Rose signed with the Cincinnati Reds after graduating from high school in 1963, and played second base. During his impressive career, Rose set several other records, including the most singles in the major leagues (3,315), most seasons with 600 or more at bats in the major leagues (17), most career doubles in the National League (746), and most career runs in the National League (2,165). He was also named World Series MVP, *Sports Illustrated*'s Sportsman of the Year, and the *Sporting News* Man of the Year.

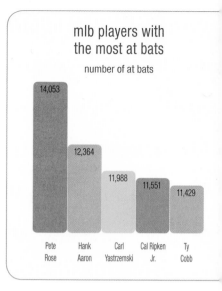

mlb players with the most at bats

number of at bats

Pete Rose	Hank Aaron	Carl Yastrzemski	Cal Ripken Jr.	Ty Cobb
14,053	12,364	11,988	11,551	11,429

mlb player with the most career RBIs

Hank Aaron

During his 23 years in the major leagues, right-handed Hank Aaron batted in an incredible 2,297 runs. Aaron began his professional career with the Indianapolis Clowns, a team in the Negro American League, in 1952. He was traded to the Milwaukee Braves in 1954 and won the National League batting championship with an average of .328. He was named the league's Most Valuable Player a year later when he led his team to a World Series victory. Aaron retired as a player in 1976 and was inducted into the Baseball Hall of Fame in 1982.

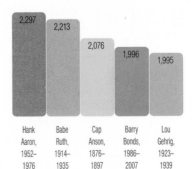

mlb players with the most career RBIs

number of runs batted in

Hank Aaron, 1952–1976	Babe Ruth, 1914–1935	Cap Anson, 1876–1897	Barry Bonds, 1986–2007	Lou Gehrig, 1923–1939
2,297	2,213	2,076	1,996	1,995

runner with the fastest mile

Hicham El Guerrouj

Moroccan runner Hicham El Guerrouj is super speedy—he ran a mile in just over 3 minutes and 43 seconds in July 1999 while racing in Rome. He also holds the record for the fastest mile in North America with a time just short of 3 minutes and 50 seconds. El Guerrouj is an Olympian with gold medals in the 1,500-meter and 5,000-meter races. With this accomplishment at the 2004 Athens Games, he became the first runner in more than 75 years to win both races at the same Olympics. El Guerrouj returned to the Olympics in 2006 as a torchbearer in Torino, Italy.

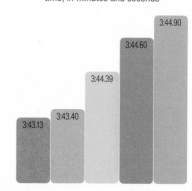

runners with the fastest mile

time, in minutes and seconds

3:43.13	3:43.40	3:44.39	3:44.60	3:44.90
Hicham El Guerrouj, Morocco	Noah Ngeny, Kenya	Noureddine Morceli, Algeria	Hicham El Guerrouj, Morocco	Hicham El Guerrouj, Morocco

top-earning female tennis player

Serena Williams

Serena Williams has earned more than $55.4 million since she began playing professional tennis in 1995. During her amazing career, Williams has won 61 singles championships and 22 doubles championships, as well as three gold medals in the 2000, 2008, and 2012 Olympics. She has also won all four of the Grand Slam championships and holds 18 of those titles. Williams has won many impressive awards, including AP's Female Athlete of the Year, the BBC's Sports Personality of the Year, and two ESPY Awards.

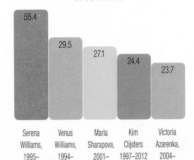

top-earning female tennis players

career earnings, in millions of US dollars

Serena Williams, 1995–	Venus Williams, 1994–	Maria Sharapova, 2001–	Kim Clijsters, 1997–2012	Victoria Azarenka, 2004–
55.4	29.5	27.1	24.4	23.7

top-earning male tennis player

Roger Federer

Tennis great Roger Federer has earned $81.2 million since his career began in 1998. He has won 78 singles titles and 8 doubles titles, including 17 Grand Slams. His major victories include four Australian Opens, one French Open, six Wimbledon titles, and five US Opens. From February 2, 2004, to August 17, 2008, Federer was ranked first in the world for 237 consecutive weeks. He is also the only player in history to win five consecutive titles at two different Grand Slam tournaments (Wimbledon and US Open).

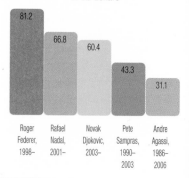

top-earning
male tennis players

career earnings, in millions
of US dollars

81.2	66.8	60.4	43.3	31.1
Roger Federer, 1998–	Rafael Nadal, 2001–	Novak Djokovic, 2003–	Pete Sampras, 1990–2003	Andre Agassi, 1986–2006

woman with the most grand slam singles titles

Margaret Court Smith

Margaret Court Smith won 24 Grand Slam singles titles between 1960 and 1975. She is the only woman ever to win the French, British, US, and Australian titles during one year in both the singles and doubles competitions. She was only the second woman to win all four singles titles in the same year. During her amazing career, she won a total of 64 Grand Slam championships—more than any other woman. Court was the world's top-seeded female player from 1962 to 1965, 1969 to 1970, and 1973. She was inducted into the International Tennis Hall of Fame in 1979.

women with the most grand slam singles titles

number of titles won

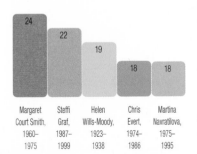

Margaret Court Smith, 1960–1975	Steffi Graf, 1987–1999	Helen Wills-Moody, 1923–1938	Chris Evert, 1974–1986	Martina Navratilova, 1975–1995
24	22	19	18	18

man with the most grand slam singles titles

Roger Federer

Swiss tennis great Roger Federer has won a record 17 Grand Slam championship titles and earned more than $81 million since he turned pro in 1998. He has four Australian Open wins, one French Open win, seven Wimbledon wins, and five US Open wins. Federer is also one of only two players to win the Golden Slam—winning all four Grand Slam championships and an Olympic gold medal in the same year (2008). Federer achieved his 17th Grand Slam title when he defeated Andy Murray at the Wimbledon gentleman's final in 2012.

men with the most grand slam singles titles
number of titles won

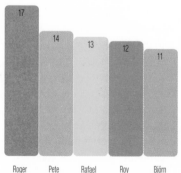

Roger Federer, 2003–	Pete Sampras, 1990–2002	Rafael Nadal 2001–	Roy Emerson, 1961–1967	Björn Borg, 1974–1981
17	14	13	12	11

mls player with the most game-winning goals

Jeff Cunningham

Jeff Cunningham has scored 40 game-winning goals during his career. The Jamaican forward turned pro in 1998 and began his career with the Columbus Crew. He has also played with Real Salt Lake, Toronto FC, and FC Dallas. Cunningham has played in 365 games for a total of 22,751 minutes. He has scored a total of 134 goals and is tied for first for most career goals scored in the league. Cunningham is a two-time MLS Golden Boot winner (2006 and 2009), and has been named to the MLS XI team three times (2002, 2006, and 2009). He's appeared in 22 post-season matches, and scored 5 play-off goals.

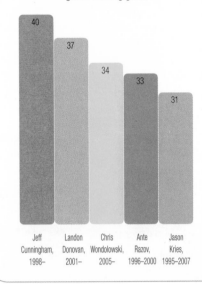

mls players with the most game-winning goals

game-winning goals

Jeff Cunningham, 1998–	Landon Donovan, 2001–	Chris Wondolowski, 2005–	Ante Razov, 1996–2000	Jason Kries, 1995–2007
40	37	34	33	31

woman with the most CAPS

Kristine Lilly

With a total of 352, Kristine Lilly holds the world record for the most international games played, or CAPS. This is the highest number of CAPS in both the men's and women's international soccer organizations. She has a career total of 130 international goals—the second highest in the world. In 2004, Lilly scored her 100th international goal, becoming one of only five women to ever accomplish that feat. Lilly was named US Soccer's Female Athlete of the Year three times (1993, 2005, 2006). She retired in January 2011.

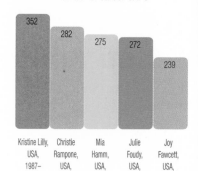

women with the most CAPS

number of career CAPS

Kristine Lilly, USA, 1987–2011	Christie Rampone, USA, 1997–	Mia Hamm, USA, 1987–2004	Julie Foudy, USA, 1988–2004	Joy Fawcett, USA, 1987–2004
352	282	275	272	239

man with the most CAPS

Ahmed Hassan

Ahmed Hassan, the captain for the Egyptian national soccer team and a midfielder for the Egyptian Premier League's Zamalek SC, has the most CAPS—or international games—with 184 appearances. He made his international debut in 1995. Hassan helped the National team win four CAF Africa Cup of Nations between 1998 and 2010, and was named the tournament's best player twice. He has also played in the Belgium Cup, the Turkish Cup, and the CAF Championship League. In 2010, Hassan was voted Best African-Based Player of the Year.

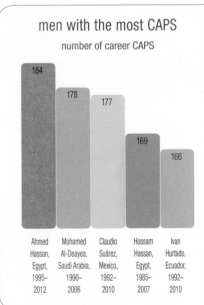

men with the most CAPS
number of career CAPS

Ahmed Hassan, Egypt, 1995–2012	Mohamed Al-Deayea, Saudi Arabia, 1990–2006	Claudio Suárez, Mexico, 1992–2010	Hossam Hassan, Egypt, 1985–2007	Ivan Hurtado, Ecuador, 1992–2010
184	178	177	169	166

country with the most world cup points

Germany

Germany has accumulated a total of 37 points during World Cup soccer competition. A win is worth 4 points, runner-up is worth 3 points, third place is worth 2 points, and fourth place is worth 1 point. Germany won the World Cup four times between 1954 and 2014. Most recently, Germany earned 4 points for a first-place finish in 2014. The World Cup is organized by the Fédération Internationale de Football Association (FIFA) and is played every four years.

countries with the most world cup points

total number of points

37	31	25	17	10
Germany/ W. Germany, 1954–2014	Brazil, 1958– 2014	Italy, 1934– 2006	Argentina, 1978– 2014	Uruguay, 1930– 1950

*As of August, 2014

driver with the most formula one wins

Michael Schumacher

Race-car driver Michael Schumacher won 91 Formula One races in his professional career, which began in 1991. Out of the 250 races he competed in, he reached the podium 154 times. In 2002, Schumacher became the only Formula One driver to have a podium finish in each race in which he competed that season. He won seven world championships between 1994 and 2004. Schumacher, who was born in Germany, began his career with Benetton but later switched to Ferrari. He retired from racing in 2006.

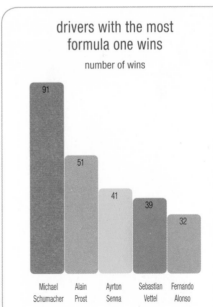

drivers with the most formula one wins

number of wins

Michael Schumacher	Alain Prost	Ayrton Senna	Sebastian Vettel	Fernando Alonso
91	51	41	39	32

driver with the fastest daytona 500 win

Buddy Baker

Race-car legend Buddy Baker dominated the competition at the 1980 Daytona 500 with an average speed of over 177 miles (285 km) per hour. It was the first Daytona 500 race run in under three hours. Baker had a history of speed before this race—he became the first driver to race more than 200 miles (322 km) per hour on a closed course in 1970. During his amazing career, Baker competed in 688 Winston Cup races—he won 19 of them and finished in the top five in 198 others. He also won more than $3.6 million. He was inducted into the International Motorsports Hall of Fame in 1997.

drivers with the fastest daytona 500 wins

average speed, in miles (kilometers) per hour

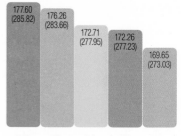

177.60 (285.82)	176.26 (283.66)	172.71 (277.95)	172.26 (277.23)	169.65 (273.03)
Buddy Baker, 1980	Bill Elliott, 1987	Dale Earnhardt, 1998	Bill Elliott, 1985	Richard Petty, 1981

Jimmie
Johnson

driver with the most consecutive sprint cup championships

Jimmie Johnson

Jimmie Johnson has won five consecutive Sprint Cup Championships between 2006 and 2010. With his 54 series wins, he is ranked 10th in career victories. During his career, Johnson has also had 138 top-five finishes and 208 top-ten finishes. He has been named Driver of the Year four times, which is a record he holds with teammate Jeff Gordon. Johnson joined the Hendrick Motorsports team in 2002, and drives a Chevrolet owned by Gordon. In addition to his Sprint Cup victories, Johnson has won the Daytona 500 one time and the Coca-Cola 500 and the All State 400 three times each.

drivers with the most consecutive sprint cup championships

consecutive wins

Jimmie Johnson, 2006–2010	Cale Yarborough, 1976–1978	Jeff Gordon, 1997–1998	Dale Earnhardt 1993–1994	Darrell Waltrip 1981–1982
5	3	2	2	2

highest-paid NASCAR driver
Dale Earnhardt Jr.

In 2012, NASCAR driver Dale Earnhardt Jr. won $25.6 million. This total includes race winnings, as well as income earned for several endorsements including Wrangler, Chevrolet, and Dollar General. During his career, he has won more than $100 million. Earnhardt drives the number 88 Chevy Impala for Hendrick Motors in the NASCAR Sprint Cup Series. He's competed in more than 450 NASCAR Sprint Cup races and 120 NASCAR Nationwide Series races during his 16-year career. Earnhardt Jr. has 19 career wins, and 108 top-five finishes. He won the Daytona 500 in 2004, and the Busch Series Championship in 1998 and 1999.

highest-paid NASCAR drivers
earnings in 2013, in millions
of US dollars

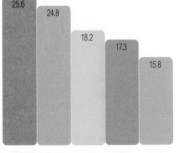

Dale Earnhardt Jr.	Jimmie Johnson	Jeff Gordon	Tony Stewart	Kyle Busch
25.6	24.8	18.2	17.3	15.8

rider with the most superbike race points

Josh Herrin

Josh Herrin accumulated 345 superbike race points during the 2013 season. Herrin, an American who raced for Monster Energy Graves Yahama, won races at four venues during the season—Daytona National Speedway, Mid-Ohio Sports Car Course, Miller Motorsports Park, and New Jersey Motorsports Park. He also had 5 second-place finishes in 2013. Herrin first competed in superbike during the 2012 season, where he finished in fourth place after 14 top-5 race finishes.

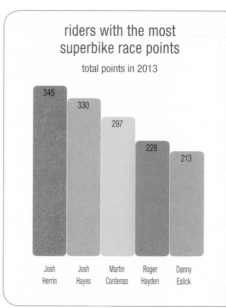

riders with the most superbike race points
total points in 2013

Josh Herrin	Josh Hayes	Martin Cardenas	Roger Hayden	Danny Eslick
345	330	297	228	213

rider with the most motocross world titles

Stefan Everts

Stefan Everts is the king of motocross with a total of ten world titles. He won twice on a 500cc bike, seven more times on a 250cc bike, and once on a 125cc bike. During his 18-year career, he had 101 Grand Prix victories. Everts was named Belgium Sportsman of the Year five times. He retired after his final world title in 2006 and is now a consultant and coach for the riders who compete for the KTM racing team.

riders with the most motocross world titles

number of wins

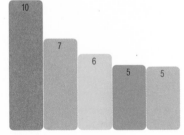

Stefan Everts, Belgium	Joel Robert, Belgium	Antonio Cairoli, Italy	Roger De Coster, Belgium	Eric Geboers, Belgium
10	7	6	5	5

jockey with the most triple crown wins
Eddie Arcaro

Between 1938 and 1961, jockey Eddie Arcaro won a total of 17 Triple Crown races. Nicknamed "the Master," Arcaro won the Kentucky Derby five times, the Preakness six times, and the Belmont six times. He holds the record for the most Preakness wins, and is tied for the most Kentucky Derby and Belmont wins. He was also horse racing's top money winner six times between 1940 and 1955. During his career, Arcaro competed in 24,092 races and won 4,779 of them.

jockeys with the most triple crown wins

number of wins

Eddie Arcaro	Bill Shoemaker	Bill Hartack	Earl Sande	Pat Day
17	11	9	9	9

nhl team with the most stanley cup wins

Montreal Canadiens

The Montreal Canadiens, also known as the Habs, won an amazing 24 Stanley Cup victories between 1916 and 1993. That's almost one-quarter of all the Stanley Cup championships ever played. The Canadiens were created in December 1909 by J. Ambrose O'Brien to play for the National Hockey Association (NHA). They eventually made the transition into the National Hockey League. Over the years, the Canadiens have included such great players as Maurice Richard, George Hainsworth, Jacques Lemaire, Saku Koivu, and Emile Bouchard. The Canadiens started strong in the 2014 NHL Playoffs, but were defeated in Eastern Conference finals.

nhl teams with the most stanley cup wins
number of stanley cup wins

Montreal Canadiens	Toronto Maple Leafs	Detroit Red Wings	Boston Bruins	Edmonton Oilers
24	13	11	6	5

nhl player with the most career points

Wayne Gretzky

Wayne Gretzky scored an unbelievable 2,857 points and 894 goals during his 20-year career. Gretzky was the first person in the NHL to average more than two points per game. Many people consider Canadian-born Gretzky to be the greatest player in the history of the National Hockey League. In fact, he is called "The Great One." He officially retired from the sport in 1999 and was inducted into the Hockey Hall of Fame that same year. After his final game, the NHL retired his jersey number (99). In 2005, Gretzky became the head coach of the Phoenix Coyotes.

nhl players with the most career points

number of points scored

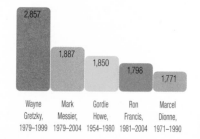

Wayne Gretzky, 1979–1999	Mark Messier, 1979–2004	Gordie Howe, 1954–1980	Ron Francis, 1981–2004	Marcel Dionne, 1971–1990
2,857	1,887	1,850	1,798	1,771

nhl goalie with the most career wins

Martin Brodeur

Not much gets by goalie Martin Brodeur—he's won 688 games since he was drafted by the New Jersey Devils in 1990. Still playing with the Devils, Brodeur has helped the team win three Stanley Cup championships. He is also the only goalie in NHL history to complete seven seasons with 40 or more wins. Brodeur has been an NHL All-Star ten times. He has received the Vezina Trophy four times and the Jennings Trophy five times. He also ranks first in the league in regular-season shutouts.

nhl goalies with the most career wins
number of games won

Martin Brodeur, 1991–	Patrick Roy, 1984–2003	Ed Belfour, 1988–2007	Curtis Joseph, 1989–2009	Terry Sawchuck, 1945–1970
688	551	484	454	447

nhl player with the most power play goals

Dave Andreychuk

Dave Andreychuk has scored more power play goals than any other player in NHL history with 274. A power play occurs when one team has all five players on the ice, and the other team has at least one player in the penalty box. The full-strength team has a huge advantage to score with the extra player on the ice. Andreychuk was in the NHL from 1982 to 2006, and played for the Buffalo Sabres, the Toronto Maple Leafs, the New Jersey Devils, the Boston Bruins, the Colorado Avalanche, and the Tampa Bay Lightning. With a total of 1,338 points, he is one of the highest-scoring left wings in NHL history.

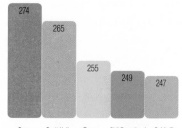

nhl players with the most power play goals

power play goals

Dave Andreychuk, 1982–2006	Brett Hull, 1985–2006	Teemu Selanne, 1988–2014	Phil Esposito, 1964–1981	Luc Robitaille, 1986–2006
274	265	255	249	247

305

nhl player with the most overtime winning goals

Jaromir Jagr

Jaromir Jagr works well under pressure—he has 18 overtime winning goals during his 23-year NHL career. He has a career point total of 1,755 and was the fifth overall draft pick in 1990. Currently a Boston Bruin, Jagr has also played for the Pittsburgh Penguins, the Washington Capitals, the New York Rangers, the Philadelphia Flyers, and the Dallas Stars. He also has two Olympic medals, and—in 1991 and 1992—he helped the Penguins win the Stanley Cup.

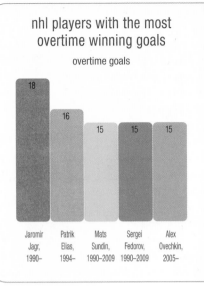

nhl players with the most overtime winning goals

overtime goals

Jaromir Jagr, 1990–	Patrik Elias, 1994–	Mats Sundin, 1990–2009	Sergei Fedorov, 1990–2009	Alex Ovechkin, 2005–
18	16	15	15	15

highest-paid hockey player
Sidney Crosby

In 2013, Sidney Crosby earned $16.5 million through his NHL salary and endorsements. The Pittsburgh Penguins pay Crosby $12 million per year, and he banked another $4.5 million in endorsements for Reebok, Gatorade, and Bell. The Canadian center was the first overall draft pick in 2005, and was the captain of the gold-medal-winning Team Canada at the 2010 Olympic Games. He holds several NHL records, which include being the youngest player voted to the starting lineup in an All-Star Game, and the youngest player to reach 200 career points.

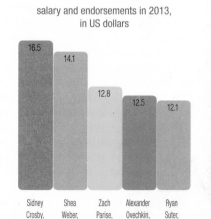

highest-paid hockey players
salary and endorsements in 2013, in US dollars

Sidney Crosby, Pittsburgh Penguins	Shea Weber, Nashville Predators	Zach Parise, Minnesota Wild	Alexander Ovechkin, Washington Capitals	Ryan Suter, Minnesota Wild
16.5	14.1	12.8	12.5	12.1

307

Index

311

Photo Credits

Dreamstime; 128: iStockphoto/Thinkstock; 129: ESRI/ AP Images; 130: Gerard Lacz/Animals Animals; 131: Courtesy Ministry for Primary Industries; 132: Photomyeye/Dreamstime; 133: Media Bakery; 134: Tony Ludovico/AP Images; 135: Tom Brakefield/Media Bakery; 136: Visuals Unlimited/Corbis Images; 137: Jens Kuhfs/Getty Image; 138: Gail Johnson/Dreamstime; 139: Jan Martin Will/Shutterstock, Inc.; 140: Datacraft/ UIG/age fotostock; 141: Brian Grant/Dreamstime.com; 142: Keith Begg/Corbis Images; 143: Yva Momatiuk & John Eastcott/Minden Pictures; 144: Andras Deak/ iStock/Thinkstock; 145: Oleg Znamenskiy/Dreamstime; 146: Roughcollie/Dreamstime; 147: Sylvain Cordier/ Biosphoto; 148: Ryszard Laskowsk/Dreamstime; 149: Fuse/Thinkstock; 150: Javarman/Dreamstime; 151: Gerrit De Vries/Dreamstime; 152: PICANI/imagebroker/ age fotostock; 153: Dr. P. Marazzi/Photo Researchers; 154: David A. Northcott/Corbis Images; 155: Joe McDonald/Corbis Images; 156: Joe McDonald/Corbis Images; 157: Visuals Unlimited, Inc./Dave Watts/Getty Images; 158: minphotos061676 - Cyril Ruoso/Minden Pictures/Newscom; 159: Andrew Murray/Nature Picture Library; 160: Driverjcs/Dreamstime; 161: Franco Banfi/ Getty Images; 162: Pete Oxford/Minden Pictures; 163: Dave Massey/Dreamstime; 164: Martin Shields/Alamy Images; 165: Deborah Hewitt/Dreamstime; 166: Dompr/ Dreamstime; 167: Nagel Photography/Shutterstock, Inc.; 168: Linn Currie/Shutterstock, Inc.; 169: Feng Wei Photography/Getty Images; 170: Alexey Fedorov/ Thinkstock; 171: Staffan Widstrand/Corbis Images; 172: Juan Manuel Barreto/AP Images; 173: Mareandmare/ Shutterstock Inc.; 174: Suzanne Long/Alamy Images; 175: Frank Krahmer/Media Bakery; 176: William Perry/ Dreamstime; 177: George McCarthy/Corbis Images; 178: Kira Kaplinski/Dreamstime; 179: Beisea/Dreamstime; 180: Corbis Images; 181: Phil Coale/AP Images; 182: Roberto Borea/AP Images; 183: Bill Greenblatt/UPI/ Landov; 184: imagegallery2/Alamy Images; 185: Lloyd Cluff/Corbis Images;

US RECORDS:

186: Medioimages/Photodisc/Thinkstock; 187 top: Franck Fotos/Alamy Image; 187 bottom: psnaturephotography/ Thinkstock; 188 top: JoMo333/Shutterstock, Inc.; 188 bottom: Jupiterimages/Thinkstock; 189 top: Phil Schermeister/Alamy Images 189 bottom: Zack Frank/ Shutterstock, Inc.; 190: William Manning/Corbis Images; 191: Mark A. Johnson/Corbis Images; 192: Ron Adcock/ Dreamstime; 193: Belliot/Dreamstime; 194: Geri Lavrov/ Getty Images; 195: Tony Sweet/Media Bakery; 196: Courtesy Lake Compounce; 197: Smallbones/Wikipedia; 198: Jeff Kinsey/Dreamstime; 199: Courtesy Georgia Sports Hall of Fame; 200: Roger Ressmeyer/Corbis Images; 201: iStockphoto/Thinkstock; 202: Courtesy University of Illinois at Urbana-Champaign Library; 203: CEFutcher/iStockphoto; 204: Kim Pin Tan/Dreamstime; 205: Scott T. Smith/Corbis Images; 206: AP Images; 207: Todd Landry photography/flickr/Getty Images; 208: Layne Kennedy/Corbis Images; 209: Wikipedia; 210: Kevin Fleming/Corbis Images; 211: Andrew Horne/Wikipedia; 212: Bill Ross/Corbis Images; 213: Philip Gould/Corbis Images; 214: James A. Finley/AP Images; 215: Gabbro/ Alamy Images; 216: Bill Grant/Alamy Images; 217:

Michael Valdez/iStockphoto; 218: Zentilia/Shutterstock, Inc.; 219: Bob Krist/Corbis Images; 220: Steve Hamblin/ Alamy Images; 221: Patrick Batchelder/Alamy Images; 222: iStockphoto/Thinkstock; 223: Gary Greff; 224: Scott Witte/Courtesy Kalahari Resorts; 225: John Elk III/Getty Images; 226: Bruce Shippee/Dreamstime; 227: Darlene Bordwell; 228: Bob Krist/Corbis Images; 229: Yalonda M. James/Post and Courier/AP Images; 230: Tom Bean/ Corbis Images; 231: Don Klumpp/Alamy Images; 232: Bob Levey/Getty Images; 233: Leon7/Wikipedia; 234: Capecodphoto/iStockphoto; 235: Mollie Bailey/The Chronicle of the Horse; 236: George White Location Photography; 237: Jacek Jasinski/Shutterstock, Inc.; 238: Troppmann/Wikimedia; 239: Robert Nickelsberg/Getty Images;

SPORTS:

240: Tom DiPace/PACET/AP Images; 241 top: Ethan Miller/Getty Images; 241 bottom: Suzanne Plunkett/ Reuters; 242 top: Jonathan Ferrey/Getty Images; 242 bottom: Kyodo/AP Images; 243 top: Noah Graham/NHLI via Getty Images; 243 bottom: Bob Thomas/Popperfoto/ Getty Images; 244: Martin Rose/Bongarts/Getty Images; 245: Richard Bord/Getty Images; 246: John Berry/Getty Images; 247: Ragnar Singsaas/Getty Images; 248: Jim Bourg/Reuters/Corbis Images; 249: Beth A. Keiser/AP Images; 250: Bettmann/Corbis Images; 251: Alan Diaz/ AP Images; 252: USA TODAY Sports/US Presswire; 253: Richard Mackson/Getty Images; 254: Bill Baptist/ WNBAE/Getty Images; 255: MCT via Getty Images; 256: Andrew D. Bernstein/NBAE/Getty Images; 257: Noah Graham/NBAE via Getty Images; 258: Cal Sport Media via AP Images; 259: Philip James Corwin/Corbis Images; 260: Jeffrey Phelps/AP Images; 261: Greg Fiume/ Corbis Images; 262: Denis Poroy/AP Images; 263: Al Behrman/AP Images; 264: Hans Deryk/AP Images; 265: Ronald Martinez/Getty Images; 266: Jonathan Daniel/ Getty Images; 267: Mark Humphrey/AP Images; 268: Jorge Guerrero/AFP/Getty Images; 269: Michael Cohen/ Getty Images; 270: Scott Halleran/Getty Images; 271: Alan Diaz/AP Images; 272: Duomo/Corbis Images; 273: Reuters/Corbis Images; 274: Thearon W. Henderson/ Getty Images; 275: Denis Poroy/AP Images; 276: Ron Heflin/AP Images; 277: Wally McNamee/Corbis Images; 278: Bettmann/Corbis Images; 279: MLB Photos via Getty Images; 280: Harry Harris/AP Images; 281: Reuter/ Corbis Images; 282: John O'Boyle/Corbis Images; 283: David J. Phillip/AP Images; 284: Bettmann/Corbis Images; 285: Bettmann/Corbis Images; 286: Francois Lenoir/Reuters/Corbis Images; 287: Rick Stevens/AP Images; 288: Alan Diaz/AP Images; 289: Mike Lawn/Fox Photos/Getty Images; 290: Kyodo via AP Images; 291: Jamie Sabau/Getty Images; 292: Kevork Djansezian/ AP Images; 293: Ben Curtis/AP Images; 294: Jean-Yves Rusznewski/TempSport/Corbis Images; 295: Fritz Reiss/ AP Images; 296: AP Images; 297: Reinhold Matay/ AP Images; 298: Jerome Miron/USA TODAY Sports Images; 299: Mirco Lazzari gp/Getty Images; 300: Gert Eggenberger/AP Images; 301: Jim Wells/AP Images; 302: David E. Klutho/Sports Illustrated/Getty Images; 303: Bettmann/Corbis Images; 304: Bill Kostroun/AP Images; 305: Ryan Remiorz/AP Images; 306: Cal Sport Media via AP Images; 307: Joe Sargent/NHLI via Getty Images.

SCHOLASTIC SUMMER READING CHALLENGE™

WWW.SCHOLASTIC.COM/SUMMER

KIDS ANSWERED THE CHALLENGE!

Kids from every state in the US and 29 countries around the world participated in the **2014 Scholastic Summer Reading Challenge**.

From May 5 to September 5, 2014, they logged the minutes they spent reading in an effort to set a NEW world record in the ultimate reading challenge:

Read for the World Record!

CONGRATULATIONS TO ALL STUDENTS WHO HELPED SET THE RECORD!

Total minutes read from May 5 to September 5, 2014: **304,749,681**

Millions of Reading Minutes

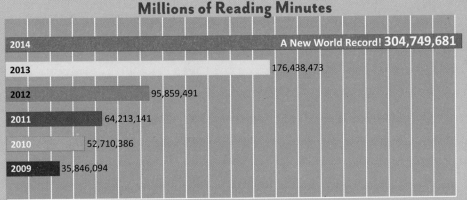

Year	Minutes
2014	A New World Record! 304,749,681
2013	176,438,473
2012	95,859,491
2011	64,213,141
2010	52,710,386
2009	35,846,094

0 15 30 45 60 75 90 105 120 135 150 165 180 195 210 225 240 255 270 285 300

SCHOLASTIC SUMMER READING CHALLENGE™

CHECK OUT THESE COOL FACTS:

TOP 20 STATES WITH THE MOST MINUTES READ:

1.	Florida	77,402,944
2.	Texas	57,443,905
3.	North Carolina	15,153,741
4.	New Jersey	11,038,696
5.	New York	10,871,417
6.	Louisiana	10,088,648
7.	California	8,942,745
8.	Pennsylvania	6,988,342
9.	Michigan	5,462,003
10.	Virginia	5,287,376
11.	Ohio	4,076,529
12.	Kentucky	4,015,908
13.	Wisconsin	3,654,525
14.	Minnesota	3,622,977
15.	South Carolina	3,616,997
16.	Illinois	3,229,868
17.	Washington	2,895,860
18.	Massachusetts	2,776,133
19.	Colorado	2,480,091
20.	Maryland	2,148,563

STATES WITH THE MOST MINUTES READ

Did your state make the top 20?

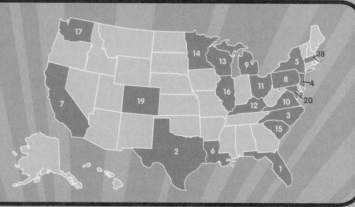

STUDENTS FROM AROUND THE WORLD PARTICIPATED!

Schools from 29 countries added minutes to the new world record. Three international schools read enough minutes to rank in the top 100 worldwide: Our Lady of Mercy School, Rio de Janeiro, Brazil (#6); NPS International School, Singapore (#58); and Seoul Foreign School, Seoul, South Korea (#73). Top countries included:

Brazil	China	Japan	Singapore	Spain
Canada	Dubai	Malaysia	South Korea	Uzbekistan

THE TOP SUMMER READING SCHOOL IN THE WORLD!

Top honor in the 2014 Scholastic Summer Reading Challenge goes to **Boggy Creek Elementary School** in Kissimmee, Florida, whose students read **10,925,325** minutes toward Read for the World Record!

Members of Boggy Creek Elementary School with their minutes.

ROUNDING OUT THE TOP 20 SUMMER READING SCHOOLS!

These schools round out the top 20 list and are recognized for their outstanding contribution toward setting the new world record:

Sun Valley Elementary	Monroe, NC	7,440,636
Jackson Elementary School	McAllen, TX	7,360,626
Beacon Cove Intermediate School	Jupiter, FL	7,062,077
Liberty Park Elementary School	Greenacres, FL	6,299,927
Our Lady of Mercy School	Rio de Janeiro, Brazil	4,721,405
Lake Nona Middle School	Orlando, FL	4,444,734
Heritage Elementary School	Greenacres, FL	4,208,329
Kenner Discovery Health Sciences Academy	Kenner, LA	4,126,669
Flora Ridge Elementary School	Kissimmee, FL	3,837,367
Ballantyne Elementary School	Charlotte, NC	3,534,504
Hunters Creek Elementary School	Orlando, FL	3,376,499
Reedy Creek Elementary School	Kissimmee, FL	3,334,409
Carroll Academy	Houston, TX	3,227,495
Newell Elementary School	Allentown, NJ	3,106,854
St. Aloysius Catholic School	Baton Rouge, LA	2,977,510
Oakridge Middle School	Clover, SC	2,795,663
Hill Intermediate School	Houston, TX	2,738,671
Odom Elementary School	Houston, TX	2,492,952
Bussey Elementary School	Houston, TX	2,471,933

Total number of participating schools:

7,311

Total number of students who logged minutes:

276,426

406 schools logged **100,000** minutes or more!

TOP SCHOOLS IN EACH STATE!

These schools all earned top state school honors by reading the most in their state or district.

Valley Intermediate School	Pelham, AL	Spoede Elementary School	Saint Louis, MO
Chugiak Elementary School	Chugiak, AK	Roosevelt Elementary School	Great Falls, MT
Scott L. Libby Elementary School	Litchfield Park, AZ	Centura Public School	Cairo, NE
The New School	Fayetteville, AR	Kirk L. Adams Elementary School	Las Vegas, NV
Warm Springs Elementary School	Fremont, CA	Broken Ground Elementary School	Concord, NH
Franklin Elementary School	Centennial, CO	Newell Elementary School	Allentown, NJ
Scotland Elementary School	Scotland, CT	Vista Grande Elementary School	Rio Rancho, NM
St. Anne's Episcopal School	Middletown, DE	Village Elementary School	Hilton, NY
Dupont Park Adventist School	Washington, DC	Sun Valley Elementary School	Monroe, NC
Boggy Creek Elementary School	Kissimmee, FL	Turtle Creek-Mercer Elementary School	Turtle Lake, ND
Savannah Country Day School	Savannah, GA	Wyandot Run Elementary School	Powell, OH
Holy Family Catholic Academy	Honolulu, HI	Northeast Elementary School	Owasso, OK
Peregrine Elementary School	Meridian, ID	Holy Cross Catholic School	Portland, OR
Glenn Elementary School	Normal, IL	Oil City Middle School	Oil City, PA
Traders Point Christian Academy	Whitestown, IN	Oak Lawn Elementary School	Cranston, RI
Clayton Ridge Elementary School	Guttenberg, IA	Oakridge Middle School	Clover, SC
Heatherstone Elementary School	Olathe, KS	Creek Side Elementary School	Spearfish, SD
Veterans Park Elementary School	Lexington, KY	Crosswind Elementary School	Collierville, TN
Kenner Discovery Health Sciences		Jackson Elementary School	McAllen, TX
Academy	Kenner, LA	Riverview Elementary School	Saratoga Springs, UT
Telstar Middle School	Bethel, ME	Calais Elementary School	Plainfield, VT
Glenallan Elementary School	Silver Spring, MD	Ashburn Elementary School	Ashburn, VA
Halifax Elementary School	Halifax, MA	Highlands Elementary School	Renton, WA
Rawsonville Elementary School	Ypsilanti, MI	North Elementary School	Morgantown, WV
Parkview Elementary School	Rosemount, MN	Hillcrest Elementary School	Chippewa Falls, WI
Annunciation Catholic School	Columbus, MS	Pronghorn Elementary School	Gillette, WY

MILLION MINUTE READERS CLUB!

More schools than ever reached the million-minute mark in 2014. Outside of the top 20 schools, students at these schools reached this awesome milestone.

Calvert Elementary School	Houston, TX	2,106,620
Thacker Avenue Elementary School	Kissimmee, FL	2,047,758
Sunset Palms Elementary School	Boynton Beach, FL	1,849,812
Ashburn Elementary School	Ashburn, VA	1,784,908
Timber Trace Elementary School	Palm Beach Gardens, FL	1,752,391
Raymond Academy	Houston, TX	1,701,081
Dovalina Elementary School	Laredo, TX	1,673,827
Rayford Road Intermediate School	Humble, TX	1,652,855
Potowmack Elementary School	Sterling, VA	1,553,200
Heatherstone Elementary School	Olathe, KS	1,518,111
Hickory Creek Elementary School	Jacksonville, FL	1,490,574
Warm Springs Elementary School	Fremont, CA	1,476,120
Gray Elementary School	Houston, TX	1,464,253
Carmichael Elementary School	Houston, TX	1,429,132
Worsham Elementary School	Houston, TX	1,389,569
Goodman Elementary School	Houston, TX	1,339,445
Stephens Elementary School	Houston, TX	1,336,250
Francis Elementary School	Houston, TX	1,312,744
Veterans Park Elementary School	Lexington, KY	1,291,844
Marcella Intermediate School	Houston, TX	1,272,710
Holy Ghost Catholic School	Hammond, LA	1,123,941
Johnson Elementary School	Houston, TX	1,117,183
Hillcrest Elementary School	Chippewa Falls, WI	1,114,628
Harris Academy	Houston, TX	1,109,863
Don Juan Avila Elementary School	Aliso Viejo, CA	1,104,379
Village Elementary School	Hilton, NY	1,069,516
Lexington Creek Elementary School	Missouri City, TX	1,060,610
Partin Settlement Elementary School	Kissimmee, FL	1,023,980